Places to Go with ~~Children~~ *little wons*
in Northern California

dear littlewon,
i couldn't resist
picking up this book
for us to share. i
Thought iT would make a
nice partner for our
restaurant Guide. i hope
we can find Time To visit
each place Thats right
for us. let's geT
sTarted soon, ok?
HAPPY CHRISTMAS
1982,
Love, Louis

Places to Go with Children *little wons* ~~Children~~
in Northern California

Elizabeth Pomada

CHRONICLE BOOKS/SAN FRANCISCO

Needless to say, this book was not done by just one person.
I must say "Thank you" to Lauren and Jennifer, Elizabeth and
Deborah, Diana and Marc, Eric and Chris, Cindy and Christopher and Alan, our "test" children. But most of all, thank
you to my editor, chauffeur, idea man, hero, and the biggest
child of them all—MFL.

E. P.

Library of Congress Cataloging in Publication Data

Pomada, Elizabeth.
   Places to go with children in northern
California.

   Includes index.
   1.   California—Description and travel—
1951-   —Guide-books.   I.   Title.
F859.3.P58   1980   917.94'0453   80-10140

Cover photograph by Janet Fries

Chronicle Books
870 Market Street
San Francisco, CA 94102

TABLE OF CONTENTS

INTRODUCTION

To research the first edition of PLACES TO GO WITH CHILDREN IN NORTHERN CALIFORNIA, we explored, read books, and drove over most of Northern California, searching out places that would be educational, historical, and, as the Pollardville Ghost Town billboard puts it, "entertational." We believe that if you and your children can learn something and have fun at the same time, then the good time is worth twice as much. Most of the places listed here are enjoyable no matter how old you are.

In updating the book, we again traveled through Northern California. We learned that the book *Roots* and the Bicentennial made people more aware of their history. They wanted to share their past with their children. Many museums—the Depot in Sonoma, the San Joaquin Historical Museum in Lodi, Calaveras County's museum in San Andrea, Rio Vista's museum, Healdsburg's museum and Old Town in Eureka—were created or enriched by historical societies spurred on by the celebration of 1976.

Traveling through Northern California you'll find a wonderfully varied, beautiful country—and learn the history of the state at the same time. This book concentrates on places to go, rather than on things to do, so we haven't included the usual activities youngsters like, such as bowling, skateboarding, skiing, pool, skating, go-carting, miniature golf, ballooning, and ice skating. Nor have we included all the national, state, county, and city parks.

We give special emphasis to year-round attractions—and to those that are free. There are some well-known tourist attractions that were left out because we feel they are either not suitable or not especially enjoyable for children.

Museums, steam railroads, natural wonders, special restaurants that appeal to youngsters, and man-made amusements are all here for you to try—along with a list of festivals, fairs, and feasts that are annual happenings.

Local Chambers of Commerce, tourist offices, or a telephone call can give you up-to-the-minute times, prices, and dates, as well as lodging and driving information. Most attractions are privately owned and subject to changes in schedules and prices at any time. Most places are closed on Christmas, Thanksgiving, and New Year's Day. All chapters are planned so that you can drive from place to place in order, radiating out from San Francisco. Do call first if you're going a long way.

We'd like to hear about special places you and your children discover. In the meantime, equipped with this book and your imagination, you and your children are sure to have a glorious time. Enjoy!

(Please note that throughout the book the abbreviations GGNRA and SHP are used for Golden Gate National Recreation Area and State Historic Park respectively.)

1

SAN FRANCISCO

What is the secret of San Francisco's attraction? A combination of natural beauty, a short but lively history in which gold and disaster loom large, and a dynamic mixture of peoples and cultures: Hispanic, Chinese, Italian, Russian, French, Japanese. Together, these elements have made a magnet that attracts visitors from all over the world.

San Francisco is a center for culture (and counterculture), business, education, entertainment, and tourism. The City provides a lot to see and do for children and their parents. And those formidable hills notwithstanding, the best way for a family to do it is on foot (with sweaters on hand in case of fog or winds). So pick an area and a destination, park the car or get off one of the ubiquitous buses, and start walking!

For openers, we suggest taking a cable car to the Fairmont Hotel on Nob Hill, and the free ride on its outside elevator to the Crown Room at the top. Night or day, the view is spectacular. From there, walk through North Beach, with its exciting Italian delicatessens, to the Bay, where you'll find something for everyone. For a 360-degree view of the Bay and the City, stop by at Coit Tower on the top of Telegraph Hill. The observation platform at the top of the tower is 210 feet high (open daily, 9 to 4:30, 50¢).

On the other side of town, the first twelve blocks of Clement Street is the heart of the Russian District. Nosh a piroshki, a tasty meat-filled pastry, as you wander through neighborhood stores. The Mission District offers Latin American groceries and a multitude of Mexican delights. For kids, just as for adults, the neighborhoods of San Francisco offer glimpses of other cultures.

And as my nephew Alan says "Just riding the cable cars up and down hills and looking is the best thing to do."

CALIFORNIA DIVISION OF MINES & GEOLOGY MINERAL EXHIBIT

Room 2022, The Ferry Building (at the foot of Market Street). (415) 557-0633. Mon.–Fri., 8 to 4:30. Free.

If you like all kinds of rocks, this is the place for you. It has many-colored rocks, phosphorescent rocks, a giant piece of salt and quartz, big gold pieces, gold dust, ore and nuggets. A five-foot-high model of a quartz mill shows how gold is extracted from ore and another model shows the workings of the Idaho-Maryland gold mine. There are also display cases for every county in the state, showing minerals to be found in each.

GOLDEN GATE FERRY TO LARKSPUR OR SAUSALITO

Next to the Ferry Building (at the foot of Market Street). (415) 332-6600. Ferries leave the City daily, at 1½ hour intervals. Call for schedule. Adults: $2, children, $1.

The Golden Gate Ferry leaves its slip at the foot of Market Street, passes Alcatraz Island, and docks across the bay. The shop on board serves good coffee and snacks —and the views are wonderful!

12

VAILLANCOURT FOUNTAIN

Embarcadero Plaza, at the foot of Market Street. Free.

When the water in this bizarre, poured-concrete fountain is turned off, it "looks like it was hit by an earthquake but didn't fall all the way down." But when the water is running and you can walk over, under, and around rushing falls and streams, it's another story. Embarcadero Plaza hosts an informal crafts fair on weekday lunch hours and on weekends. Next door, the Hyatt Regency offers a spectacular twenty-first century lobby to wander around, with a fountain, a burbling brook, and glass elevators that travel—up to the top of the lobby—twenty stories above.

DOLPHIN P. REMPP SHIPBOARD RESTAURANT

Embarcadero and Berry, Pier 42. (415) 777-5771/ 957-1470. Dinner, Tues.-Sat.

The three-masted, 155-foot long cargo schooner *Ellen* has been transformed to a flag-flying restaurant perched on San Francisco's Embarcadero. A nautical bar and stainless steel galley serve fresh seafood and drinks to people who like to "pretend cruise" while they dine.

A WORLD OF OIL/CHEVRON USA

555 Market Street. (415) 894-4895. Mon.–Fri. 9 to 4. Tours of the building by appointment. 25-minute film weekdays at noon. Free.

If you've ever wondered how oil is found, produced, transformed into thousands of products, and used for energy, heat, and lubrication, this is the place to come. The multi-media program starts with a short film showing how tremendous amounts of time and underground pressure change decomposing plants and animals into petroleum, and how oil was obtained and used in the past. The search for black gold is illustrated with photos, models of rigs, actual drilling tools, and a mural of a modern refining plant. Three life-size dioramas show the role oil has played in American life. One with particular appeal for children shows a family in a 1910 kitchen.

THE OLD MINT

Fifth and Mission Streets. (415) 556-3630. Tues.–Sat., 10 to 4. 1½ hour guided Tours by appointment. Closed on holidays. Free.

A half-hour film, "The Granite Lady," unfolds this history of California and the part the Old Mint played in it, from the crackling excitement of the Gold Rush to the terror of the earthquake and fire. Visitors can see tokens, notes, walrus and seal skins and other forms of money as well as a stack of seventy-one gold bars, and gold nuggets. In one of the restored rooms, the superintendent's office, the clock reads "Time is Money." Visitors can strike their own souvenir medal on an 1869 coil press.

LYLE TUTTLE'S TATTOO MUSEUM

30 Seventh Street. (415) 864-9798. Tues.–Sat., 12 to 6. Free.

Thousands of tattoos, designs and instruments, including a Bear War (1898) tattoo pattern and pre-Columbian tattoo devices, makes this one of the most unusual museums in the world.

THE ASAWA FOUNTAIN

Hyatt Hotel on Union Square (Stockton Street, between Sutter and Post). Free.

Ruth Asawa, creator of the Mermaid Fountain in Ghirardelli Square, has given the people of San Francisco a one-stop tour of the people and places that make up the City. This round (14 feet in diameter) fountain, on the steps of the hotel's plaza, was molded in bread dough—the same dough children use for sculpting—and cast in bronze. And the little people, trees, Chinese dragon, gingerbread houses, and school buses demand to be touched. If you stand at the bottom of the fountain, you'll find the Ferry Buiding; then as you go around the fountain counter-clockwise, you'll see Coit Tower, Broadway, Maritime Park, the Cannery, the zoo, the Mission District—everything laid out in the same general direction as it is in real life. A group of Noe Valley schoolchildren created one of the fountain's forty-one plaques, which depicts the children of San Francisco. Your children will enjoy figuring out which one it is.

VICTORIA STATION RESTAURANT

Embarcadero at Broadway. (415) 433-4400 Mon.–Fri., 11:30 to 2, 5:30 to 11. Fri. & Sat. until 12.

A fascinating complex of dining rooms made up of old railroad cars form this popular steak and prime rib restaurant. Authentic railroad furnishings and memorabilia create an atmosphere especially entertaining for kids. Each meal begins at Platform #1, the free baggage-cart salad bar. Other Victoria Stations can be found at Larkspur Landing, Sunnyvale, Sacramento, Burlingame, Oakland, and Lake Tahoe. Prices are moderate to expensive.

ENERGY EXPO

Pacific Gas & Electric. 77 Beale Street, Mezzanine. (415) 781-4211 x 4248. Mon.–Fri., 9 to 4:30. Groups by appointment. Free.

Multi-media shows explain nuclear power and planning amid fourteen exhibits exploring energy: how electricity is made; sources of natural gas; undersea ecology; and more. Visitors can run a model of one of the first electric generators, simulate an energy dispatcher, and operate wind and solar energy models.

MUSEUM OF MONEY OF THE AMERICAN WEST

Bank of California, 400 California Street, downstairs. (415) 765-0400. Mon.–Thurs., 10 to 3; Fri. until 5. Free.

This small but beautifully mounted collection of money and gold provides intriguing glimpses of banking and mining in the Old West. Privately minted coins from Utah, Colorado, and California illustrate the kind of money used before the U.S. Mint was established in San Francisco. Ingots, bullion, fiscal paper, currency, and early bank drafts are here, along with counterfeit coins and counterfeit detectors. (One method of counterfeiting was "the platinum menace,"—hollowing coins and filling them with platinum, which was then worth much less than gold.) A new addition to the museum's collection is the pair of pistols used in a duel between David S. Terry and David C. Broderick in 1859.

WELLS FARGO HISTORY ROOM

420 Montgomery Street. (415) 396-2619. Banking days, 10 to 3. Free.

A Wells Fargo Concord Stagecoach is the centerpiece of this history of Wells Fargo and the Old West. Treasure boxes and old money, iron doors from the Wells Fargo building in the gold-country town of Chinese Camp, "The Pioneer's Ten Commandments," samples of gold, a map of Black Bart's twenty-eight stagecoach robberies (the story goes that he was always polite to women), and many other items provide details of Western history. Early photographic methods are illustrated, with sample photos and cameras and the high seat and iron headrest used for daguerrotypes.

There's even a Buffalo Bill collection, along with a huge collection of stamps and postmarks.

LEVI STRAUSS HISTORY ROOM

2 Embarcadero Center Lobby. (415) 544-6000. Mon.–Fri., 10 to 4. Free.

Memorabilia of "the pants that won the West," photos of Levi's first customers—the loggers, gold miners, cowboys and railroad workers—and a display of original canvas and denim Levis will fascinate any jeans wearer.

CHINATOWN WAX MUSEUM

601 Grant Ave. (415) 392-1011. 10 a.m.-11 p.m., daily. Adults $1.50; ages 6–12, $1. Group discounts.

The Chinese Wax Museum, the only wax museum in the United States devoted to Chinese history, presents thirty-one authentic-looking scenes that capture the traditions, customs and pageantry of China and San Francisco's Chinatown. You find Marco Polo meeting Kublai Khan, a classic Chinese opera frozen in mid-song, a traditional Chinese wedding, a dinner for immigrant Chinese on board a Gold Rush ship, and a court lady's boudoir. I don't recommend the aisle of burial and torture scenes—and you can easily circumvent it by moving directly from the grocery store to the herb shop that displays acupuncture charts and needles—but many youngsters do seem to have a fascination with death and my eleven-year-old nephew liked the grisly details a lot better than I did. My favorite scene is the Chinese New

Year parade and celebration dragon. A visit takes about forty-five minutes and is worth the price of admission.

CHINATOWN

Walking through Chinatown can be like walking in another country or it can simply be a shopping trip, depending upon your mood. For the curious, there are fortune cookie factories, fish stores, and temples. Fortune cookie making is not a romantic process. A row of tiny griddles revolves under a hose that squirts dough onto each pan. The pans continue their circle, cooking the dough on their way to the fortune cookie-maker. She picks up the browned wafer, pushes it onto a spur to give it the first fold, inserts the paper fortune, presses the final fold, and puts the cookie into a muffin tin to harden. *Golden Gate Fortune Cookie Co. (23 Ross Alley, above Grant, between Washington and Jackson, 781-3956)* and *Lane Hueng Fortune Cookie Factory (1507 Grant)* frequently leave their doors open so you can poke your head in to see the process in action. If you plan to go as a group, make an appointment. *The King Chow Temple (Clay and Stockton, above the post office on the fourth floor)* is the oldest Chinese family association in the U.S. Visiting hours are posted on the door. *T'ien Hou Miao Temple (125 Waverly Place, fourth floor, 10-5 and 7-9 p.m. daily)* is dedicated to the Queen of Heaven and boasts a ceiling filled with carved wood mythological figures. In nearby Portsmouth Square, there's a small wooden house leading to one of the best slides in the city.

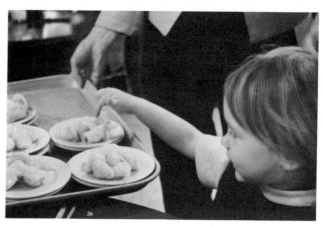

Jennifer chooses a shrimp dumpling at Yank Sing.

YANK SING RESTAURANT

671 Broadway. 781-1111. 10-5 daily.
Yank Sing is our favorite *dim sum* restaurant. *Dim sum*, also called Chinese tea or Chinese breakfast, means "heart's delights," and is one of the nicest ways I know of to have brunch. *Dim sum* is simply little bites of good things. A waitress or waiter comes around with a huge tray, from which you choose small plates of such delicacies as steamed pork buns, curry cakes, beef dumplings, shrimp rolls, black-bean sauce spareribs and barbecued pork sandwiches. You pay by the number of plates piled up on your table, so if a dish like shrimp balls comes on two plates, and there are just 2 or 3 of you, you can ask for half an order, or one plate's worth. That way you'll have more room to try more "heart's delights."

16

CHINESE HISTORICAL SOCIETY OF AMERICA

17 Adler Place (between Grant and Columbus, just south of Broadway). Tues.–Sun., 1-5. Donation.

Chinese societies throughout California have contributed to this small, almost hidden museum to show how Chinese contributed to California's development. Ceremonial swords, printing blocks, an altar block, porcelain pillows, clothes worn by nineteenth century highborn and laborers, opium pipes, photos, and documents crowd the walls.

NORTH BEACH MUSEUM

1435 Stockton. (415) 391-6210. Mon.–Thur., 9-4:30; Fri. until 6; Sat., 9-1 (upstairs in Eureka Federal Savings Bank). Free. Tours by appt.: 334-4600.

Photographs and artifacts in changing thematic exhibits rejoice in the City's, particularly North Beach's, colorful past, from the Gold Rush to the Earthquake, to the Beat Generation. On our last visit, we saw an exhibit of San Francisco's mayors, from the *alcaldes* of the 1830s to the present.

MUSEO ITALO AMERICANO

512 Union St., (415) 788-9266. Wed.–Sun., 12-4, and by appointment. Free.

Italian and Italo-American culture are the focal points here. A twenty-foot time line on one wall shows the development of art and architecture from the Renaissance to today. Changing exhibits include ancient Roman artifacts and the art of present-day artist Sam Provenzano.

CABLE CAR BARN MUSEUM

Washington and Mason Streets, (415) 474-1887. 10-5:45 daily. Donation. Closed holidays.

All three cable car lines in San Francisco are run by the huge revolving red and yellow wheels in the brick cable car barn, built in 1887. Visitors can watch the wheels from a gallery, where there are samples of the cable itself and charts explaining how the cable cars work. Scale models, earthquake mementoes, old cable car seats, and photographs mix with the cable cars on display, including the first one to operate in San Francisco, in 1873.

PIONEER HALL, SOCIETY OF CALIFORNIA PIONEERS

456 McAllister Street. (415) 861-5278, Mon.–Fri., 10-12 and 1-4. Closed holidays and during July and August. (Children under 16 must be with adult.) Free.

Photos of the 1906 San Francisco earthquake and fire and the 1915 Exposition fill rack after rack in this long room. There is also a free slide show about the earthquake. Artifacts of the gold miners, of the transcontinental railroad and the driving of the Golden Spike, and menus used in early railroad dining cars are in wall cases. The Vigilence Committee Bell, Vallejo's campaign chest, artifacts from the Niantic, fire trumpets, and an old stagecoach are among the other items of interest.

SAN FRANCISCO MUSEUM OF MODERN ART

Veterans Memorial Building, Van Ness at McAllister. (415) 863-8800. Tues., Wed. and Fri., 10-6; Thurs. until 10 p.m.; weekends, 10-5. Closed holidays. Adults $2; under 16, $1. Group rates.

The modern art museum constantly changes its exhibits of paintings, sculpture, works of art on paper, and photography. During a recent visit, we saw a dazzling collection of rock posters from the sixties.

Across the street, in City Hall, there's a changing mini-museum where you can buy a Cable Car medal, early stocks and bonds, or other historical memorabilia. (Mon.–Fri., 8:30-4:30, 558-2525. Free.)

HAAS-LILIENTHAL HOUSE

2007 Franklin (between Washington & Jackson). (415) 441-3004. Guided tours Wed. 12-4, Sun., 11-4:30. Adults $2, students, seniors and groups, $1.

This glorious Queen Anne Victorian, built in 1886, is a completely furnished memory of yesteryear. There's even a cat snoozing on the dining room sofa!

HIPPO HAMBURGERS

2025 Van Ness. (415) 771-3939. 11 a.m.-2:30, Fri. and Sat. until 3 a.m.

There are fifty-five kinds of hamburgers to choose from in this cheerful, circus-like restaurant. There are Italian burgers, onion-burgers, Hawaiian burgers, Tahitian burgers and Cannibal burgers at prices ranging from $3. The children's menu offers a Giraffeburger, Rhinoburger, and Gorrillaburger ($1.55). Sandwiches, guacamole, divine fried onion rings, and good desserts such as warm banana fritters topped with hot cinnamon sauce, round out the menu. The adventurous might try the "nudeburger"—a roll-less hamburger smothered in ice cream, hot fudge, chopped nuts, a cherry and a pickle. Hippo bibs, lollipops and balloons are there for the asking, and birthday boys and girls will be energetically sung to.

GHIRARDELLI CHOCOLATE MANUFACTORY

Ghirardelli Square, North Point and Polk, 11:30-10 daily. (415) 771-4903.

Since the beginning of the century, Ghirardelli Stone-ground Chocolate has been a popular trade name throughout the West. This red brick, aromatic ice cream and candy shop invokes that name in a nostalgic corner of the old Ghirardelli factory. After filling out an order form and paying the cashier, you locate a marble-topped table, then take turns watching the chocolate-making machinery in the back of the room until your order number is called. The Emperor Norton and Golden Gate Banana Splits are $2.75. Twin Peaks is chocolate and vanilla ice cream under marshmallow and chocolate sauce, covered with a whipped cream fog. The best buy may be the hot chocolate ($1), a large mug of ambrosial chocolate topped with melting marshmallows or whipped cream.

Ghirardelli Square is a nice place to spend an afternoon. You can browse through Japanese, Dutch, Finnish, Mexican, Greek, and American stores; taste almonds, watch street artists, delight in the kite store, dine in Indian, Mexican, Mandarin, Hungarian or Italian restaurants, or just sit and watch the sailboats on the bay.

NATIONAL MARITIME MUSEUM AT SAN FRANCISCO (GGNRA)

Foot of Polk St. (415) 556-8177. 10-5 daily, until 6 in summer. Free.

The Maritime Museum is a mecca for ship lovers of all ages. The maritime history of San Francisco lives here in models of clippers, British iron ships, schooners, barkentines, cutters, cod fishers; and in photos, figureheads, tools, scrimshaw, guns and harpoons, diaries, and ships' logs. The 19-foot sloop "Mermaid," which one man sailed from Osaka to San Francisco, is on the porch. Billy Bones, Blackbeard, Mary Read, and Anne Bonny are some of the pirates standing at the entrance to the Steamship Room. Inside, you'll find models of the *Queen Mary* and various cargo and warships from World War I to the present.

SAN FRANCISCO HISTORIC SHIPS AT HYDE STREET PIER (GGNRA)

556-6435, 10-5 daily, open longer hours in summer. Free. Tours and Environmental Living Programs by appointment.

Plastic wands tell you about the ships, with narrations dramatized by sounds of creaking timbers, whistles and the cries of seagulls as you climb aboard a sailing lumbership or the last paddle-wheel ferry to operate on

San Francisco Bay. *The C. A. Thayer* operated here as a salmon packet and then as a codfisher. You can go below decks to see the captain's cabin (he sometimes brought his wife) and the galley, and then get behind the wheel. *The Eureka* features a display of antique cars and trucks on her lower deck. Upstairs, there's a newsstand stocked with all of the 1920 magazines and candies. Our favorite thing is the old nickelodeon. For 25¢ you can dance through the cavernous, empty vessel to the tunes of yesteryear. A paddle-steam tug that operated on the Thames, *The Eppleton Hall*, has just been added to the pier, along with *The Alma*, the last remaining San Francisco Bay scow schooner, and *Hercules*, a 1907 ocean-going steam tug. *The Arc*, a Victorian houseboat, and the Tubs Building, a cordage company, are being restored.

WHARF WAX LIFE MUSEUM

275 Jefferson. (415) 885-5656. Sun.–Thurs., 10-10, Fri. and Sat. until 12. Adults, $2; ages 5-12, $1.

There's something here for every age group: twenty-seven exhibits peopled by one hundred leaders in world history and literature. The Tin Man, Hansel and Gretel, Rip Van Winkle, Frankenstein and Dracula, Emperor Norton, and Jackie Onassis seem ready to come alive.

THE WORLD OF THE UNEXPLAINED

235 Jefferson. (415) 673-9765. Sun.–Thurs., 10-10, Fri. and Sat. until 12. Adults $3, under 12, $1.50.

Psychic phenomena, the fourth dimension, extra-terrestrial life, ESP, Kirlian photography, witchcraft, magic and mystery are explored here. There are masks, dolls, amulets, exhibits of psychokinesis and the lives of plants, and assorted other challenges to our imaginations. A walk through the Magic Shop can also be fun.

RIPLEY'S BELIEVE IT OR NOT! MUSEUM

175 Jefferson. (415) 771-6188. Sun.–Thurs., 10-10; Fri. and Sat. until 12. Adults, $3.50; under 12, $1.75.

Over twenty-five hundred oddities and puzzles are displayed along the Crooked Lane that leads you through this amusing collection. A man with four pupils in his eyes, another covered in chains, and another with a hole in his head gave us pause, as did the two-headed goat, the log cabin made with Lincoln pennies, and the display of "dressed" fleas. Curious children will think this is a perfect place to spend a rainy afternoon.

THE WINE MUSEUM OF SAN FRANCISCO

633 Beach. (415) 673-6990. Tues.–Sat., 11-5; Sun., 12-5. Free. Closed holidays. Children must be accompanied by adults.

The story of wine in art, quotable quotes, sculpture, history, and mythology is nicely laid out for comfortable browsing. The Franz W. Sichel glass collection in back includes glasses dating back to Roman times as well as one said to have been used by Queen Elizabeth I.

THE DESSERT COMPANY OF SAN FRANCISCO

The Cannery. 2801 Leavenworth. (415) 928-4503. 11-11 Sun.–Thurs.; until 12 on weekends.

Fantasies are fulfilled at the Dessert Company. For $2.95, you can choose three flavors of ice cream and then head for the Dessert Bar, where you can choose from sixteen toppings—hot fudge and caramel, marshmallow, crushed oreos, spiced apples, nuts, cherries, whipped cream—and do it yourself. You can even go back for more toppings as many times as you like. Coffee, tea, straight sodas, sundaes and creations, and cakes from the best bakeries in town are there for the less adventuresome. And everyone will enjoy the view, which stretches from Berkeley to the Golden Gate.

The Cannery itself is an old fish cannery remodeled into a galaxy of shops, a movie theater, a gourmet food shop, and restaurants. Street musicians and a glass elevator in the courtyard add to the youngsters' enjoyment of the place.

WAX MUSEUM AT FISHERMAN'S WHARF

145 Jefferson. (415) 885-4975. 10-10 daily, longer hours in summer. Adults, $4.50; children and seniors, $2.

Four levels of 275 figurines in 74 scenes vie for your attention here. Princess Grace, Queen Elizabeth and Emperor Hirohito pay court to the visitor, as do movie stars such as Marilyn Monroe and Elvis Presley, and people from fables, like Peter Pan and Snow White. John Sutter drinks in an 1848 San Francisco saloon, while Emperor Norton broods in a corner. The chamber of horrors is really horrible.

OLD SAN FRANCISCO CABLE CAR RIDE

Jefferson and Mason Streets. (415) 885-4834. 10-10 daily, later in summer. Adults $1.75; seniors and ages 6-13, $1.

Follow the red brick road to the pretty cable car and ride through San Francisco's history. One hundred and fifty animated characters sing you as you travel through the Gold Rush days to the building of the City, to the Barbary Coast, to the scary 1906 earthquake and fire, and finally to the elegant Pan-Pacific Exposition and fireworks!

BALCLUTHA (GGNRA)

Pier 43. (415) 982-1886. 9 a.m.-10:30 p.m. daily. Adults, $2; ages 12-17, $1; ages 6-12, 25¢ (with parent, free).

One of the last surviving square-rigged Cape Horners, the *Balclutha* once flew twenty-five sails on its seventeen trips 'round the Horn. Today, you can spin the wheel, visit the "slop chest" and galley, check out the captain's quarters, with its plush red settee and swinging bed, ring bells, and read sea chanties and rousing tales of the Barbary Coast in the museum downstairs. The rolling of the boat on the water adds just the right touch to your imaginary cruise.

COMMODORE HELICOPTOR TOURS

Pier 43 (415) 981-4832. Mill Valley office: 332-4482. 10 a.m. to sunset daily, weather permitting. Adults $7.50; under 10, $4 for four minute Bell Jet Ranger ride. Charter rates available.

This exciting 125 mph ride swoops over Alcatraz, out onto the Bay and over the City for some great views. Be sure to bring your camera.

HELICOPTOURS

Pier 46 (shuttle from Ghirardelli Square). (415) 495-3333. Daily, weather permitting. Five tours last from seven minutes to a half hour and range in price from $8 to $48. Children under ten, half price.

ALCATRAZ ISLAND

Pier 43. (415) 546-2805. Tours every 45 min. by reservation only, 9-3 in winter, until 5:15 in summer. Adults, $2, ages 5-11, $1.

Wear walking shoes and bring a sweater on this educational, fascinating-yet-depressing tour. One friend calls the tour a sure-fire way to stop juvenile delinquency.

Nature Expeditions (328-6572) takes you on day-long teaching trips to the Farallon Islands, weekends in summer.

BAY CRUISE

Pier 43½. (415) 546-2810. Tours begin at 10 a.m. daily, weather permitting. Adults $4.50, 5-11, $2.50.

On a sunny day in San Francisco, there's nothing nicer for all of the family than the 75-minute cruise on San Francisco Bay. The guide points out special sites and buildings and tells their story, but the really important thing is the passage around that beautiful bay. You go from bridge to bridge, past Alcatraz and along the Embarcadero.

Harbor Tours leave Pier 41 to Sausalito from 7:55 a.m. to 7 p.m., arriving 35 minutes later and returning to San Francisco seven times a day. The first boats start later on weekends and holidays.

Harbor Tours also offers Sunday brunch cruises from April to October, at 10:30 and 12:30, weather permitting, by reservation. The cruise lasts one-and-one-half hours and features a buffet with a complimentary glass of champagne for adults for $11.

TIBURON—ANGEL ISLAND STATE PARK FERRIES

Pier 41, Tour information: (415) 546-2815; Island information: 435-1915. Round trip, $4.25 adults, $2.25, ages 5-11. Boats leave San Francisco at 10, 12, 2 and 3:45 daily for Angel Island and Tiburon from June 1 to Labor Day, and on weekends and holidays (except Thanksgiving, Christmas & New Years).

The Red and White Fleet crosses the Bay from Fisherman's Wharf to the romantic inlet at Angel Island. A snack bar is available, but most people spend the time on board staring at the bay and the seagulls following. For a description of Angel Island, see page 22. During the week, the ferry goes from the Ferry Building to Tiburon at 7:30 a.m. and then at 4:24, 5:15, 5:45 and 7:10. The boat leaves Tiburon to dock at the Ferry Building at 6:50, 7:30, and 8:10 a.m. then 5 and 6:30 p.m. Boats dock at Fisherman's Wharf when they leave Tiburon at 5:55 and 8 p.m.

PIER 39

The Embarcadero. (415) 981-PIER. Shops: 10:30-8:30; Restaurants, 11:30-11:30.

The entire family will enjoy the Palace of Fun Arts which welcomes you to Pier 39. Here you'll find bumper cars, a new two-story carousel, and a 25¢ arcade with games of skill and machines to play. The kids can spend hours here while you shop in the 105 stores. There are high divers, jugglers and street entertainers to amuse you. Windsurfing and sailing lessons are available, or you can rent a boat yourself (School of Sailing, 421-1725), or take a scenic one-and-one-quarter hour Bay cruise on the Blue & Gold Fleet. Neptune's Palace (434-2260) offers Lunch & Launch or Brunch & Launch combinations. If you'd rather choose your own lunch spot on Pier 39, there are twenty-three restaurants to choose from: Mexican, Japanese, Chinese, Italian, Swiss, and fish of every kind, all with fabulous views of the bay.

COST PLUS

2552 Taylor Street. (415) 673-8400. Mon.–Sat. 10-9, Sun. 11-7.

Three large, crowded stores and a garden nursery offer many hours of contented browsing. The furniture store stocks rugs from India, furniture from Mexico, and wickerware. The Arts & Antiques building specializes in interesting old posters, jewelry, and statuary from the Far East. The main building is crowded with baubles and bangles, cookware, candles, boxes, toys, trinkets, ethnic foods and exotic clothes, all reasonably priced for little pocketbooks.

S.F. FIRE DEPT. PIONEER MEMORIAL MUSEUM

655 Presidio (between Pine and Bush), (415) 861-8000. Thurs.–Sun., 1-5 and by appointment. Free.

Awe-inspiring photos of today's fire fighters mingle with uniforms, bells, trophies and mementos of men and machines, the silver speaking trumpet, leather buckets, a buffalo-leather fire hose and other relics of yesteryear. Lillie Coit, the darling of the S.F. Fire Dept., has her own case full of mementos. A 1912 fire chief's buggy, an Ahrens-Fox Piston Pumper and an 1890 American LaFrance Steam Fire Engine fill the room.

CALIFORNIA HISTORICAL SOCIETY

2090 Jackson St. (415) 567-1848. Wed., Sat. and Sun., 1-5 and by appt. Adults, $1; students and seniors 50¢. First Saturday of the month. Free.

The former Whittier Mansion features revolving exhibits of California art. En route to the second floor exhibit area, you pass through gracious drawing rooms with parquet floors, handsome fireplaces and carved wainscotting.

JAPAN CENTER

Post and Buchanan Streets. (415) 346-3242/922-6776.

The Peace Plaza, with its reflecting pools and five-tiered Peace Pagoda, is the center of many entertaining happenings through the year: festivals; music and dance programs; judo, karate and kendo matches. Inside, you can fish for an oyster with a pearl in it, have a Japanese fish pastry for dessert, and wander through bonsai, paper, gift, and book shops. The nearby blocks are filled with interesting hardware and grocery stores, tempura and sushi bars. Samarai movies and theatrical programs that will attract older children are scheduled in the corner theater. Japan Center, or "Nihonmachi" can really be another world.

FORT MASON

Marina Blvd. at Laguna. (415) 441-5705.
The Golden Gate National Recreation Area is in the process of restoring Fort Mason to active use. Thirty-five non-profit organizations reside here offering free or low-cost concerts, lectures, classes, children's hours and many support services. The San Francisco Museum of Modern Art has a wing here. *Greens* is an elegant vegetarian restaurant run by the Zen Center of San Francisco offering creative pastas and barbecues, salads picked each day at the center's Green Gulch Farm, and breads and cakes from the Tassajara Bread Bakery with a phenomenal view of the docks, the bay and Golden Gate Bridge (771-6222, lunch & dinner). Scheduled to open in Spring 1980, is the Liberty Ship *SS Jeremiah O'Brien*, a fully restored floating museum that will honor the people who made the Liberty Ships—such as the celebrated "Rosie the Riveter"—the people who sailed them, and the servicemen the ship ferried supplies and ammunition for (415) 556-3535.

OCTAGON HOUSE

2645 Gough Street. (415) 885-9796. Second and fourth Thursday of each month. Occasional Sundays. 1-4. Free.
This unusual eight-sided home is the headquarters of the Colonial Dames of America, as well as a gracious museum of Americana. A pack of Revolutionary War playing cards (with soldiers & Indians on the back), a thirteen-star flag, dishes taken into battle by the *U.S.S. Constitution* during the War of 1812 and a nineteenth-

century "mammy bench" make this a pleasantly educational stop.
Nearby Union Street offers blocks of boutiques and restaurants.

MUSEUM OF RUSSIAN CULTURE

2450 Sutter Street. (415) 921-7631. Sat., 11-3 or by appointment. Free.

A visit to this small museum will provide children with a colorful introduction to Russian culture. There are photos, letters, medals, and silks from the families of the Czars—including some funny photos of Anastasia and her sisters. Pushkin and Tolstoy, Pavlova and Nureyev, and other Russian dancers, artists, writers, and scientists are remembered here. The photos and models of Fort Ross are especially noteworthy.

SAN FRANCISCO AFRICAN-AMERICAN HISTORICAL & CULTURAL SOCIETY

680 McAllister Street. (415) 864-1010. Tues.–Sat., 10-6. Free.

African and Black American artists and inventors are honored in the exhibit hall of this cultural society. Clothing, pottery, historical documents and crafts are displayed, a library is open to students of Afro-American history. The exhibit of George Washington Carver's many uses of the peanut is a wonder, as is the one on Black American cowboys.

JOSEPHINE D. RANDALL JUNIOR MUSEUM

199 Museum Way at Roosevelt (Upper Market Street area, at 15th Street, west of Castro). (415) 863-1399. Tues.–Sat., 10-5. Free.

High on a sunny hill overlooking the city, this museum/zoo is especially designed for children. Here they can watch a seismograph, see dinosaur bones and eggs, learn about the California Indians, and pat a live chicken and pig. They can also talk to crows and mynah birds, handle various minerals and ores, and learn about electricity. During one Saturday visit, youngsters were helping to clean out the cages while two plump raccoons played on the front lawn and Puff the Iguana took an airing on the zookeeper's arm. Members of the Golden Gate Model Railroad Club, located downstairs in the building, allow the public to watch their play with the model trains on the huge room-sized track, on occasional Friday nights.

MISSION DOLORES (MISSION SAN FRANCISCO DE ASIS)

16th and Dolores. (415) 621-8203. 10-4 in winter, 9-5 in summer. 25¢ donation.

Built in 1776, the mission is San Francisco's oldest structure. The unique Corinthian and Moorish architecture is not at all like other California missions. The cemetery tells many tales.

MEXICAN MUSEUM

1855 Folsom. (415) 621-1244. Tues.–Sun., 1-5. Donation.

Prehispanic, contemporary and folk art by Mexicans and Chicanos make up the changing exhibits in this fine museum. And on the first Saturday of each month at 10 a.m., the museum sponsors a walking tour of the Mission Distrct's murals.

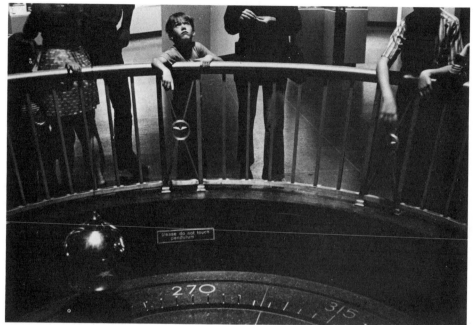

Watching the Pendulum Swing in the California Academy of Science.

GOLDEN GATE PARK

From Stanyan Street west to the ocean. (McLaren Lodge is the park's office, 588-3706.)

There are more than one thousand acres of lakes and greenery in San Francisco's Golden Gate Park and at least one hundred things to see and do. You can go boating or feed the ducks, cheer toy sailboat races, picnic, ride horses, play tennis, golf or handball, go lawn bowling, watch the grazing buffalo, bicycle, skate, watch soccer and polo matches, pitch horseshoes, shoot arrows, play cards or chess, practice your fly casting, or make water rings in the fountains. Stow Lake is the place to rent rowboats, motor boats, and pedal boats (752-0347).

The Children's Playground, on the Lincoln Ave. side of the park, features the slide with the fastest ride in the West, plus thirteen other slides, geometrical shapes to climb, and a beautiful old carousel which is being restored. There's a small animal farm there, too.

Older children might enjoy a walk through *Shakespeare's Garden* to identify the plants he wrote about, from wormwood and yew, to bilberry and eglantine.

You can climb a moon bridge in the *Japanese Tea Garden* (open 8 to dusk daily), then sit down to tea and cookies in the Japanese Tea House (30¢).

Browse through the spun-sugar Victorian *Conservatory* (9-4:30, 558-3973) at any time of year to see displays of flowers in a burgeoning, jungle-like atmosphere. Ring the Mexican Bell in the *Strybing Arboretum's Garden of Fragrance*, where you can also test your powers of smell, touch and taste (8-4:30 weekdays, 10-5 weekends, tours: 661-1316). Gaze at the *Portals of the Past*, the marble columns that are all that was left of a Nob Hill mansion after the Earthquake, and are now the guardians of a duck-filled lake. Don't forget to say thank you to John McLaren (his statute is hidden in a dell of rhododendrons across from the Conservatory—he hated statues in parks) for turning sand dunes into the greenery that graces the City.

M. H. DE YOUNG MEMORIAL MUSEUM

Golden Gate Park, north side of Music Concourse. 558-2887. 10-5 daily. Visitors 18-65, $1; 12-18, 50¢. Free first day of the month. (One admission charge admits you to the de Young, Asian Art, and the Palace of the Legion of Honor museums on the same day.)

The de Young's romantic Pool of Enchantment, with water lilies and a sculpted boy playing his pipes to two mountain lions, beckons visitors to this land of enchantment. There are paintings, sculpture, tapestries, and graphics by American, Californian and European artists. The Rembrandts are shown without fanfare and there is a lovely Mary Cassatt in the modern section. The American Wing now houses our favorite painting:

"Rainy Day in the Tropics" by Frederick Church. Children especially seem to like the "real rooms"—the muraled boudoir from Italy and the Elizabethan paneled bedrooms. A pleasant cafeteria is open for lunch and afternoon tea.

ASIAN ART MUSEUM

Golden Gate Park, next to the de Young. (415) 558-2993. 10-5 daily. Same fees and admission arrangements as the de Young.

A magnificent collection of jade is shown in a jewel box setting: the Magnin jade room. The second floor is divided among the arts of Iran, Turkey, Syria, India, Tibet, Nepal, Korea, Japan, and Southeast Asia. After looking at the beaming statues of Buddha and Kuan Yin, you can glance out picture windows to see the Japanese Tea Garden.

CALIFORNIA ACADEMY OF SCIENCE

Golden Gate Park, south side of Music Concourse. 752-8268/ 4264. 10-5 daily, winter; 9-9 daily, summer. Adults 50¢; ages 12-18, 25¢. Free admission first day of the month.

Wander through the Hall of North American Mammals, the Hall of Minerals, the Hall of North American Birds (with its model of the Farallon Island bird rookery) or head for the Hall of Fossils to see dinosaur bones, brontosaurus skulls and a whale skeleton. The Wattis Hall of Man, two African Halls, a Hall of Botany, and a Hall of Space Science lead to the third wing of the Academy.

The Powell Street Cable Car—the Best Ride in Town.

Here you'll find *Morrison Planetarium*, where a unique Sky Theater uses an Academy projector to depict the appearance of sky as seen from Earth at any time— past, present or future—on the sixty-five foot hemispherical dome. Special effects projectors take the viewer through space into whirling galaxies and black holes. Shows change regularly. For daily sky times, call 752-8268. Usually, there are shows at 2 daily, at 7:30 p.m. on Wednesday and Thursday, and at 12:30, 2, and 3:30 on weekends. Adults: $1.50; Ages 5-17, and seniors, 50¢ (under 5 by special permission). Closed Thanksgiving and Christmas. There's also a special show for everyone on weekends at 11 a.m., 50¢.

Laserium is a "cosmic" laser show in which colorful images seem to pulsate, float and dance in concert with the music against a background of stars. Shows ($3.25 for all. 752-4264) are Friday: 7:30, 9, 10:30 p.m.; Saturday: 5, 7:30, 9 & 10:30; and Sunday: 5, 7:30 & 9.

The whale fountain courtyard inhabited by crocodiles and alligators leads to the *Steinhart Aquarium* where thousands of fish, reptiles and dolphins live in 243 colorful tanks, all low enough for children to see into easily. Seahorses, deadly stonefish, dolphins that sound like Flipper, Amazon lettuce-eating manatees, piranhas, and shellfish of all colors, shapes and sizes live here. Upstairs, the *Fish Roundabout* puts you in the middle of a huge tank where fish swim quickly around you. Dolphins are fed every two hours, starting at 10:30 a.m. (Info: 752-8268).

THE EXPLORATORIUM

Palace of Fine Arts. Lyon St. (415) 563-7337. Wed. –Sun.,

1-5. Wed. 7-9:30 p.m. (summer weekends, 11-5) Groups by appointment. Closed holidays. Donations requested.

This is a do-it-yourself museum without walls where visitors are encouraged to see, touch, hear, explore, improvise, and play. Changing exhibits feature laser beams, holograms, stereophonic sound testers, radio and tv sets to take apart, and a tactile labyrinth. The Palace of Fine Arts, designed by Bernard Maybeck for the 1915 Exposition, is in one of San Francisco's most romantic spots, with ducks swimming in a beautiful lagoon outside.

PRESIDIO ARMY MUSEUM

Funston and Lincoln Blvds., Presidio. (415) 561-4115. Tues.—Sun., 10-4. Free. Groups by appt.

Founded by Spain's military forces in 1776, the Presidio has flown Spanish, Mexican and American flags. Cannons, uniforms, swords, and army memorabilia tell the Presidio's more than two-hundred-year history. Models and carefully wrought dioramas of battlefronts, the Earthquake, and the 1915 Panama-Pacific Exposition add to the interest of this museum.

Also on the Presidio is the Applied Aquatic Resources Institute (Bldg. 257, Wed.—Sun., 1-4, Free), an interpretive center demonstrating the wonderment and potential of our aquatic environment.

FORT POINT NATIONAL HISTORIC SITE

Foot of Marine Drive, under San Francisco end of the Golden Gate Bridge, on the Presidio grounds. (415) 556-1693.

10-5 daily and hourly guided tours on weekends. Free.

Nestled below the underpinnings of the Golden Gate Bridge, Fort Point, built during the Civil War, is the only brick seacoast fortress in the West—the guardian of San Francisco Bay. With the icy Pacific slamming into the retaining wall and the wind whistling around the point, this is one of the coldest spots in San Francisco. That's why the place was used as a detention barracks and "hardship tour" until World War II. Museum rooms display swords, guns, shells, chains, uniforms, handcuffs, cannon balls, an eyewitness account of the assassination of President Lincoln, relics of the San Francisco earthquake, a Confederate flag, and an old doctor's kit. And roaming through the dismal jail and barracks and through three floors of echoing hallways, discovering cannons where you least expect them, is the most fun of all.

CALIFORNIA PALACE OF THE LEGION OF HONOR

Lincoln Park, off 34th Ave. and Clement. (415) 558-2881. 10-5 daily. Adults, $1; ages 12-18, 50¢. (Same ticket counts for the Asian Art Museum and the de Young. First day of the month free admission.)

Children can explore Land's End and get a thrilling view of the Golden Gate Bridge from the ocean side here, after wandering through the impressive marble building and its rotating exhibits and collection of fine French art and twentieth century printmakers. They'll recognize Rodin's "The Thinker" sitting in the courtyard.

THE CLIFF HOUSE (GGNRA)

Land's End. (415) 751-1617. Mon.–Fri., 10-4:30; longer hours in summer.

"A drive to the 'Cliff' in the early morning . . . and a return to the city through the charming scenery of Golden Gate Park, tends to place man about as near to Elysian bliss as he may hope for in this world." B. E. Lloyd—1876. A drive to and from the Cliff House can still place you in Elysian bliss, even if the buildings themselves are getting a little ragged around the edges. It's still the best place in town to see the seals on Seal Rocks. There's a shiny new exhibit hall downstairs, showing Cliff House in its various incarnations throughout the years. And the crammed Musée Mécanique (386-1170 weekdays, 11-6; weekends, 10-7) houses more than one hundred machines, old and new, which work on small change. Swiss music boxes, a mechanical carnival, a mechanical 1920s farm, old-time movies and music machines sit alongside Star Trek, electronic games and modern cartoons. There are restaurants and gift shops upstairs.

POLLY ANN'S EXOTIC FLAVORS

3142 Noriega Street. (415) 664-2472. Daily, 12-10; Fri. and Sat. until 11.

This small, personal neighborhood ice cream shop has 270 rotating flavors of the best, the most interesting ice cream in San Francisco. American Beauty Rose (made with real American Beauty roses), Chinese Ginger, Avocado, Honeycomb, cinnamonny Chocolate Sombrero, sensuous chocolate/orange liqueur-flavored Sabra,

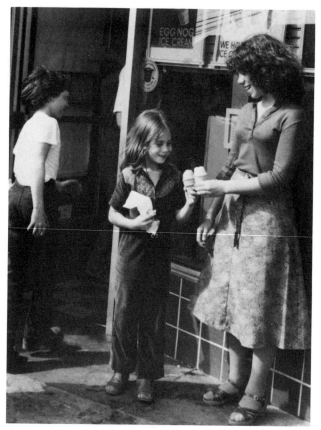

A toast—to the best ice cream in San Francisco.

Im-Peach-Mint, Piña Colada, Blue Bubblegum, Star Wars, all demand tasting. And that's just what you can do. Ted and Lee Hansen let you have tastes—cheerfully —of as many flavors as you like. And every dog and child under five gets a special cone of his own—free.

30

SAN FRANCISCO ZOO

Sloat Blvd. and the Great Highway. (415) 661-4844. 10-5 daily. Adults, $2. Seniors, 50¢, under 15, free. Free days: First Tuesday and Second Saturday of each month. Additional charge for children's zoo, merry-go-round and zoo-mobile. Zoo Key: 50¢.

Animals from all over the world live here in naturalistic settings. There are cassowary birds and wallaroos, snow leopards, okapis, spectacled bears, flamingos, seals, emus, koalas, Moulon and Barbary sheep, peacocks and reindeer. The main aviary building is a tropical rain forest where you can walk amid 85 species of birds, from pigeons to curassows (11-3 daily). "Creepers," the insect zoo, houses bird-eating spiders, ant lions, tarantulas, and black widows. We always head for the Big Cat house, where the lions and tigers are fed every day at 2 (except Monday, because in the jungle they don't eat every day). On the grounds there are spaceship rides and a cable car and locomotive to play on. And the animals in the barnyard are there to be petted. The zoo is right near the ocean, so it's wise to have sweaters handy.

PUBLIC RELATIONS TOURS

KNBR
Fox Plaza. (415) 546-2273. Free tours by appointment.

In half an hour, you can see studios, control rooms, news, sales, and FM automated equipment.

KSFO
950 California. (415) 398-5600. Free tours by appointment on one Thursday of every month.

See news production, the music library, traffic continuity, and a disc jockey in action.

KYA
1 Nob Hill Circle, Pine and Mason. (415) 391-1260. Free, by appointment.

Tours take you through broadcast studios, the control room, the news room, and FM facilities.

K-101, FM
700 Montgomery. (415) 956-5101. Tours by appointment.

See the Transamerica Pyramid while visiting this radio studio.

OLD UNCLE GAYLORD'S
2435 Mission. (415) 648-2166. Groups by appointment. Free.

The thirty-minute tour shows you the methods and equipment used to make ice cream the old way, with rock salt and ice. You'll end up in an ice cream museum that displays scoops, dishes, photographs, cranks, and signs.

2

MARIN COUNTY

MARIN COUNTY is a land of mountains and seashore, north of Golden Gate Bridge. Most of the "places" to go with children in Marin are natural wonders. You can drive to the top of Mt. Tamalpais and walk the trails overlooking miles of ocean, land and city. You can explore the silent redwood groves of Muir Woods, then travel on to Stinson or one of the lesser known beaches for a seaside picnic, rock-hunting and driftwood-collecting, or even a quick dip in the icy sea. You can also spend hours fishing in the Marin lakes, or hiking the beautiful Point Reyes National Seashore area. And when you feel the need for civilization, you can head for Tiburon or Sausalito, where the children will be as enchanted as you by the appearance and attractions of these bayside villages.

SAUSALITO

After stopping for a moment to look back at the *Golden Gate Bridge* from Vista Point, or after taking the short drive to the *California Marine Mammal Center* at the Marin Headlands Ranger Station in Ft. Cronkhite (561-7284) to see seals being cared for until they can return to their natural environment, spend a few hours in this Riviera by the Bay. Noted for years as an artist's colony, the village of Sausalito is now a mecca for tourists and young people. There are clothing and toy stores, ice cream parlors and coffee houses, art galleries and restaurants for every age, taste and budget. Visitors can climb up the stairs from Bridgeway to *The Alta Mira* (126 Harrison Ave., 332-1350, 8 a.m.-9 p.m.) for an elegant brunch and a breathtaking view of San Francisco or head for *The Spinnaker*, for lunch right out on the water (100 Spinnaker Dr., 332-1500). The *Sausalito Historical Museum*, in the old City Hall on Litho Street (Wed. and Sat., 1-5, Sun. 10-5, 332-1005) offers police and railroad memorabilia, period costumes and photos of the town since 1860. My nephew's favorite pastime, however, is simply walking along the rocks, finding baby crabs.

5/29/94 disconnected

SAN FRANCISCO BAY-DELTA MODEL

2100 Bridgeway, Sausalito. (415) 332-2871. Mon. –Fri., and First and Third Sats., 9-4, and by appointment. Free.

415
332-0334

The U.S. Army Corps of Engineers has put together a hydraulic scale model of San Francisco Bay and the Sacramento-San Joaquin Delta. The model shows the action of the tides, the flow and currents of the water, and the mixing of sea water and fresh water. Guided tours take one-and-one-half hours, but individuals can use the self-guided recorded tour system to see the exhibit at their own speed. A multi-media program presenting a history of the bay is in the works. It's a good idea to call first—the model is not always in action.

TIBURON

Named *Punta de Tiburon*, or Shark Point, by early Spanish settlers, Tiburon is a quiet, one-street bayside village, a nice place to spend a sunny afternoon. Lunch and a drink while enjoying the view from one of the many restaurants on the bay can be heaven. Nautical shops, a Swedish bakery and the bookstore are all fun to browse through. Hardy walkers can head up the hill to

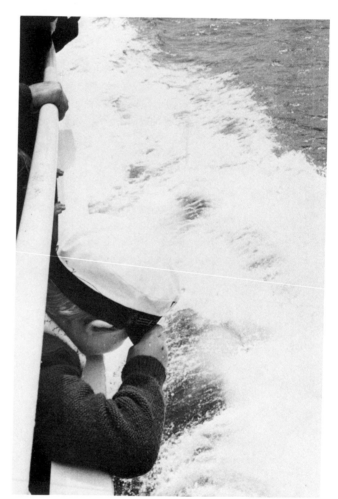

Riding the waves to Sausalito.

34

the *Landmark Society Museum in Old St. Hiliary's Church* (Sun. and Wed., 1-4, April-September and by appointment. (415) 435-1853, 50¢) to see a changing art exhibit and specimens of the local plants that grow nowhere else in the world. On the way back to Highway 101 stop at the *Lyford House*, a Victorian home maintained by the National Audubon Society as part of its wildlife sanctuary (*376 Greenwich Beach Rd., Sun. 1-4 and by appointment, 388-2524, 50¢*). Youngsters can explore the sea life and observe birds along self-guiding natural trails in the sanctuary, open Wed.–Sun., 9-5 (50¢). There are special programs and films on Sundays.

ANGEL ISLAND STATE PARK

In San Francisco Bay. (415) 435-1915. For tour information: 546-2815. For ferry information from San Francisco see page 12. Ferries leave from Tiburon hourly in summer, from 10 a.m. and weekends in winter. Adults, $1.75, children, $1. (415) 435-2131.

Secluded picnic groves, beaches, forest trails and historic military buildings under reconstruction make Angel Island a wonderful place to spend the day. An elephant train jaunts around the island (Adults, $1.50, children 75¢) to give you a good picture of these 740 acres, discovered in 1775 by Juan Manuel de Ayala. The deer are surprisingly brash.

MUIR WOODS NATIONAL MONUMENT

Off Hwy. 1, on Muir Woods Road. (415) 388-2595. Daily, 8 a.m.-sunset. Free.

This lovely forest of giant Coast redwoods, some more than two hundred feet high, is a breathtaking way to start the day. Among these magnificent trees, you'll encounter many other species of plant life—azalea, red alder and California laurels—as well as an occasional black-tailed deer scampering across the trail and, in summer, young salmon and trout swimming through Redwood Creek. Although the main inner trail of the forest is concrete, the outer trails are natural earth for easy walking. A self-guiding natural trail along the creek helps you understand the forest. A Braille Trail is provided. A lunch counter, gift shop and ranger's station are located near the park entrance.

MARIN COUNTY HISTORICAL SOCIETY MUSEUM

1125 B Street, Boyd Park, San Rafael. (415) 454-8538. Wed.–Sat. 1-4 p.m. Free.

Designed "to stir the imagination and bring back panoramas of the past" this over-stuffed, cheerful museum displays original Mexican land grants and mementos of the Miwoks, Mexicans and pioneers who settled Marin. Lillie Coit's shoes, Mrs. Berryessa's silk shawl, an early San Quentin oil lamp, and the military collection are fascinating. Our youngsters' favorite thing was the huge tallow kettle at the entrance. Once used for boiling elk tallow at the Rancho Olompali, the kettle was also used as a stewpot for the military during the Bear Flag War. Today it's a great hiding place.

Just down the block is the *Mission San Rafael Archangel (1104 5th Ave., (415) 454-8141. 11-4 daily, except Sun., 10-4. Free.)* A small display of mission furniture and spanish tapestries is in the giftshop, photos

Birdwatching at the Marin Wildlife Center.

and arrowheads and priests' garments are displayed in windows outside, and the small chapel flies the six flags under which the mission has served: Spain, Mexico, the California Republic, the United States of 1850, the Vatican, and the United States of America.

A few blocks across town, the *Marin Wildlife Center (76 Albert Park Lane, (415) 454-6961, Tues.—Sat., 10-4 donations)* is a small wildlife rehabilitation and nature education center. The animals on exhibit, such as a bear, birds, raccoon, owls and hawk, can never be released because they can no longer fend for themselves in the wilds. Dioramas of Marin County's forest, salt marsh, chaparral, seashore and grasslands exhibit the animals of the area.

AUDUBON CANYON RANCH

Hwy. 1, 3 miles north of Stinson Beach. (415) 383-1644.

Sat., Sun. and holidays, 10-4, March 1-July 4, and by appointment. Free.

This one-thousand-acre wildlife sanctuary bordering on the Bolinas Lagoon is a peaceful spot to view birds "at home." From a hilltop, you can watch the nesting activities of the Great Blue Heron and Great Egret. The ranch's pond, stream and canyon are a living demonstration of the region's ecology—the delicate balance between plant and animal life and their environment. The display hall shows local fauna and flora and information on the San Andreas fault. Picnic areas are available.

POINT REYES NATIONAL SEASHORE

Hwy. 1, Olema. (415) 663-1092. 8-sundown daily. Free.

Sir Francis Drake is said to have landed here in 1579. The beauty of the sharp cliffs, swimmable and unswimmable surf, streams, tidepools, lowlands, and forest meadows make you wonder why he went back to England. You can watch the bird rookeries in the trees and sea lion rocks just off shore. You can walk along well-marked nature trails, including an earthquake trail, hike, backpack, and camp. The information center at Olema has a small natural history exhibit and the Parks Department raises Morgan horses nearby. We like Drake's Beach best and before we set out, we call the ranger's office there (699-1250) to make sure it's sunny.

The Point Reyes Lighthouse is now open to the public, 10-5 daily, weather permitting (669-1534).

A new part of Pt. Reyes is *Kuleloklo*, the Miwok Village. Visitors can see a reconstructed sweat house and huts built with the original materials as well as artifacts such as hunting snares and sewing implements. Best of all, you can help with the reconstruction in progress during daylight hours.

Tomales Bay State Park (8-8 in summer; 8-6 in winter daily, 669-1140, $1 per car) is part of the Point Reyes National Seashore, too. Craggy Bishop pines, sandy beaches, and tidepools are the attractions here. Tidepools are the rocky pockets which retain sea-water when the tide goes out. Many strange animals and plants live among their rocks—seaweeds, anemones, barnacles, worms, jellyfish, shellfish, sand dollars, urchins, tiny fish, and algae. The best way to look at a tidepool is to lie very quietly until the tidepool's occupants think you're part of the landscape and continue to move through their daily paces. Tidepool animals may not be collected, but their activity will provide many engrossing on-the-spot hours for children and adults as well.

MARIN FRENCH CHEESE COMPANY

7500 Red Hill Rd., Petaluma (9 miles west of Novato on Novato Blvd.) (415) 762-6001. Sales room, with tasting and tour, 10-4 daily. Free.

Situated next to a pond in the rolling, cow-speckled hills between Novato and the coast, this is a perfect destination for an afternoon outing or picnic. A 15-minute tour begins with the 4,000 gallon tank of milk and takes you through the different stages of cheese making—heating the milk, adding the three "cheese" ingredients (culture, enzymes and starter), and aging. You pass shiny steel tubes and tanks, a strange Rube Goldberg-type machine that makes the cheese boxes, and different aging rooms, each with its own smell. Picnic tables are available, where you can sit and eat a picnic lunch made from ingredients available in the store.

The birds come to a Marin picnic.

MIWOK MUSEUM

2200 Novato Blvd., Miwok Park, Novato. (415) 897-4064. Tues.—Sat., 10-4 and Sun., 12-4 in summer, Sat. 10-4 in winter and by appointment. Free.

Native American artifacts are used to illustrate the prehistoric period of Marin County. Coast Miwoks are represented with decorated baskets, cooking implements, arrowheads and ceremonial charm stones shaped like fish. California plants are used for tools, food, shelter, clothing and baskets. Crafts lessons and programs are given. Picnic areas are available.

In town, the *Novato History Museum (915 de Long Ave., 897-4320, Thurs. and Sat., 10-4 except holidays, and by appointment. Free.)* focuses on the history of Rancho Novato and the pioneers. An abstract of the 1843 title to Rancho Soulajule (Rancho San Ramon), the dress and shawl of Augusta Pachero, old photographs and a wonderful old piano are the key attractions.

3

NAPA, SONOMA, AND LAKE COUNTIES

Napa, Sonoma and Lake counties are best known for the vineyards that grow on rolling hills and in the Valley of the Moon. Wineries can be fun for children to visit, not only because the wine-making process is fascinating, but because the wine industry is part of California's history and culture. In most wineries, your tour will follow the direction the grape takes, from delivery from the vineyards, to the crushing, to the aging vat, to the bottles in the tasting rooms. The listed wineries offer the most interesting plants and tours, all of which are free (including the "tasting" for the older folks). But the country itself is welcoming and seen best from the hot air balloons, gliders, planes, and parachutes now available for the brave of heart.

YOUNTVILLE-VINTAGE 1870

Hwy. 29, Yountville. (707) 944-2788. 10-5, daily.
This lovely old former winery is part of the original land grant made to Salvador Vallejo in 1838 and was bought in 1870 for $250 in U.S. gold coin. The brick exterior of the building hasn't changed much, but the interior is now a charming complex of shops, theater, candle and candy makers, potters, a glass blower and a leather craftsman, who work in open stores. The Vintage Railroad specialty shops are housed in nine authentically restored railroad cars, including two cabooses.

DOMAINE CHANDON

2280 California Drive, Yountville. (707) 944-2280. Restaurant reservations: 944-2467. 10-4:30 except Mon. and Tues.

This new star in the winery chain on Hwy. 29 makes champagne that's rosy-gold and golden-pink. The tour takes you past James Bondian huge brass vats and into musty cellars where each bottle must be turned every day by hand. The restaurant is French and very classy and the grounds, with streams and ponds, are welcoming.

ROBERT MONDAVI WINERY

Hwy. 29, Oakville. (707) 963-9611. 10:30-4:30, daily. Free.

Designed and landscaped by Cliff May, who designed the Sunset Magazine building, the Mondavi Winery offers jazz concerts and special events on summer Sundays on the center lawn.

NAPA VALLEY OLIVE OIL MANUFACTORY

End of Charter Oak Road, St. Helena, (707) 963-4173. 8-6:30 daily.

A visit to the wineries is not complete without a stop at this old-fashioned olive oil factory and sausage and cheese store. Hidden at the end of a block on the southern entrance to town, the place looks more like a deserted barn than a bustling business. Inside you'll find vast amounts of cheese, glistening pyramids of olive oil bottles, sausages and stacks of Italian delicacies. Picnic tables are available.

THE SILVERADO MUSEUM

1490 Library Ave., St. Helena. (707) 963-3757. 12-4 daily except Mon. and holidays. Free.

Robert Louis Stevenson has been associated with the Napa Valley ever since he spent a penniless honeymoon in an abandoned bunkhouse of the Silverado Mine on Mount St. Helena. Today, anyone who grew up on *A Child's Garden of Verses* or *Treasure Island* will appreciate this tribute to the man who wrote them. Portraits of Stevenson abound, including one showing him as a fair young boy with long flowing curls. Original manuscripts, illustrations, the author's toy lead soldiers, his tea set, Henry James's gloves, Robert's doll, chess set and cigarette holder, and memorabilia from the plantation in Samoa are neatly displayed in this bright new museum.

CHRISTIAN BROTHERS WINERY

Hwy. 29. St. Helena. (707) 963-2719. 10-4:30 daily. Free.

This imposing castle, the largest stone winery in the world, is the center for the good Brothers' wine aging and champagne cellar. Brother Timothy's cork screw collection is on view in the display area.

FREEMARK ABBEY

Hwy. 29, St. Helena. (707) 963-7211. Mon. –Fri. 10-5; weekends, to 6. Free.

The old Freemark Abbey Winery now houses the Hurd Beeswax Candle Factory, a small winery and gift shops, with adjoining coffee shop, restaurant and delicatessen. Weekday visitors may see the candle makers working until 4:30. On the far wall of the inside showroom, a wooden shutter opens to reveal the back of a beehive full of bees filling their honeycomb.

THE OLD BALE MILL SHP

Hwy. 29, St. Helena. 10-4:30 daily. Free.

Dr. E. T. Bale built this gristmill in 1846 and the last flour was ground here in 1879. One hundred years later, the state is restoring the mill and will soon be selling mill-ground flour to visitors who'll enjoy seeing the mill in action.

STERLING VINEYARDS

1111 Dunaweal Lane, Off Hwy. 29, Calistoga. (707) 942-5151. 10:30-4:30, except Mon. and Tues. in winter. $2.50 per person.

An aerial tramway takes visitors high into the hills to see galleries and unusual exhibits in the winery. The ride is three minutes of excitement, and there can be a long wait.

SHARPSTEEN MUSEUM AND SAM BRANNAN COTTAGE

1311 Washington St., Calistoga. (707) 942-5911, Weekends, 12-4 and by appointment.

Calistoga's romantic pioneer history comes alive in the scale model dioramas and shadow boxes. A model of Calistoga in 1865 covers one wall, others show Robert Louis Stevenson and his wife, the railroad depot (with model train) and China Camp complex, and the toll house. One of Sam Brannan's cottages (he was California's first millionaire, but died broke) has been moved to the site and refurbished right down to the ivory dressing set on the dresser. A big C & C Stage Line stagecoach stands near the front door along with a collection of hubcaps from the era of wooden spokes and gas lamps from early cars. Local artist Ben Sharpsteen donated his money, time and talent in creating this wonderful museum.

OLD FAITHFUL GEYSER OF CALIFORNIA

1299 Tubbs Lane, Calistoga. (707) 942-6463, 9 till sundown daily, weather permitting. Adults $1, under 12, 50¢, and tour discounts. Picnic area.

One of the three faithful geysers in the world, this one erupts 350-degree water about every forty minutes to heights of fifty to two hundred feet. The geyser rumbles, belches forth a small fountain, rumbles for about four more minutes, then gushes forth a rainbow of foaming steam and water. A tape gives historical and geological information and tells how geysers are formed. The owners use another geyser on the property to heat their house, and there is a wishing well nearby with 130-degree water.

THE PETRIFIED FOREST

Petrified Forest Road between Calistoga and Santa Rosa. (707) 942-6667, 9-5 daily, weekends in summer until 6. Over 10: $2.

Volcanic eruptions of Mount St. Helena six million years ago formed this forest of petrified redwoods, discovered in 1870 and written about by Robert Louis Stevenson. A lovely forest trail passes a three hundred-foot-long "Monarch" tunnel tree and "the Giant" that was already 3,000 years old when it was buried. On the way out, you'll walk through a specimen shop of fossils and petrified worms, snails, clams, nuts, and wood.

AIR PLAY

The rolling hills and soft wind currents of the area have made the skies here especially accessible. For those who are adventurous, try the following:

HOT AIR BALLOON RIDES

Great Pacific Hot Air Balloon Co., P.O. Box 656, Napa, 94558 (707) 224-4173.
Adventures Aloft, 6525 Washington St., Yountville 94599 (707) 255-8688.
AeroStat Renaissance & Ballooning Co., 1644 Silverado Trail, Napa 94558 (707) 255-6356.
Airborn of Sonoma Co., P.O. Box 789, Sebastopol 95472 (707) 823-8757. Rainbow balloon flights are $65 on weekdays per passenger, $74 on weekends.

GLIDER RIDES

Calistoga Soaring Center, 1546 Lincoln Ave., Calistoga 94515 (707) 942-5592 (plane rides, too).

PARACHUTING

Pope Valley Parachute Ranch, 1996 Pope Canyon Rd., Pope Valley 94567 (707) 965-3400.

PLANE RIDES

Bridgeford Flying Service, Napa County Airport, Napa 94515 (707) 224-0887.

PETALUMA ADOBE (SHP)

3325 Adobe Rd., Petaluma (east of Hwy. 101) (707) 762-4871, 10-5 daily. Adult ticket usable at all state parks that day, 50¢.

General Mariano G. Vallejo's ranch house, Rancho Petaluma, was built in 1836 as the centerpiece of a Mexican land grant of 66,000 acres. Here we learned that in Spanish *adobe* means, "to mix," and that the thick, naturally insulating bricks were made from clay mixed with water and straw and then dried in the sun. Visitors walk through the adobe on a self-guided tour. The kitchen, workshop, candle room, weaving room, servants' quarters and the Vallejos' living quarters upstairs are graciously furnished with some of the original pieces. Outside, there are huge iron cauldrons, clay ovens, a covered wagon, and the racks on which hides —a currency of the period—were stretched out to dry. At one time, General Vallejo had one thousand workers on the ranch, and it's not hard, standing before Rancho Petaluma today, to imagine the bustle of yesteryear.

DEPOT MUSEUM

Depot Park, between First St. E and First St. W., Sonoma (707) 938-9765 Wed.–Sun. 1-4:30. Adults 50¢, children

25¢. Free school tours by appointment.

The restored North West Pacific Railroad Station now houses a spiffy new historical museum and pioneer exhibit. The old Union Hall theater curtain, filled with ads, forms one wall. The old station master's office is now a reference library. A Victorian living room, dining room and kitchen has been created and there are grizzly bear feet, saddles, sewing machines, and an exhibit of the Native American local tribes. A box car, cattle car and gazebo are being put in order for public use. Picnic facilities are nearby, as are bocce ball courts.

SONOMA STATE HISTORIC PARK

From Third St. W and down W. Spain St. past the Sonoma Plaza to Third St. E. (707) 938-4779. 10-5 daily. Adult ticket 50¢, usable the same day at all state parks.

Lachryma Montis, at Third St. W., named after the clear spring, "Tear of the Mountain," was General Vallejo's "city house." Furnished precisely as it was when he lived there with his family—right down to the photograph of Abraham Lincoln on the wall—the house feels as if Vallejo just stepped out for a moment. One daughter's painting is on a wall, along with family photos. Behind the house is the kitchen building and the Chinese cook's quarters. The "Chalet" in front was once the storehouse and is now a Vallejo museum containing his books, pictures, saddles, coach and cattle brand, various remembrances of his family and biographies of ten of his sixteen children.

On the Plaza, you'll walk by Vallejo's first home in Sonoma. Destroyed by a fire in 1867, only the Indian servants' wing survives. You can walk through it and see a small Indian exhibit in the ranger's building. Next,

The Toscano Hotel, built in 1858, is a carefully restored mining hotel with Scott Joplin music playing in the lobby and the cards and whiskey glasses still on the tables from the century-ago players. (Tours are 10-5 daily in summer, 11-1 on Tues., and 1-4 weekends in winter.)

The Mission San Francisco Solano was the most northern and last built of the twenty-one Franciscan missions in California and the only one established under Mexican rule (1823). The padres' quarters is the oldest structure in Sonoma. Visitors can walk through the building, looking at mission exhibits, furnished rooms of the padres, spurs and leggings of the *vaqueros*, and other interesting artifacts of mission life, including a primitively painted chapel. A *ramada* is being constructed in the garden for blacksmith, weaving, breadbaking and other period crafts demonstrations.

Blue Wing Inn, across the street, was once a hotel visited by John Fremont, Kit Carson, Generals Grant, Sherman and P. Smith, and the bandit Joaquin Murietta. At present it is a complex of shops, but the state is making plans to restore it to its former glory, along with the present work on the *Sonoma Barracks*.

During your wanderings you may want to stop in at the *Sonoma Cheese Factory (2 Spain St., (707) 938-5225, 9-6 daily)* to see the young men pounding cheese bags to make Sonoma Jack, and to pick up a picnic—which you can then enjoy in the Sonoma Plaza behind *City Hall* and the *Bear Flag Monument* honoring the short-lived Bear Flag Republic. There are two fine slides in the town square playground.

BUENA VISTA WINERY

Old Winery Road, Sonoma. (707) 938-8504. 9-5 daily. *Free.*

Buena Vista was the first winery with stone cellars in California. Founded in 1857 by the Hungarian Count Agoston Haraszthy who first imported European grape varieties for commercial use, Buena Vista winery is now a California historical landmark.

SEBASTIANI VINEYARDS

389 E. Fourth Street, Sonoma. (707) 938-5532. 10-5 daily. Free.

Commemorated as one of the oldest vineyards in Northern California, Sebastiani is known for the carved oak casks and redwood tanks. Founded in 1825, this third generation winery began with a five hundred gallon tank and primitive equipment.

TRAINTOWN

Broadway, Sonoma. (707) 938-3912. 11-5:30 daily in summer; 10:30-6, winter weekends. Adults $2, children $1.25.

A fifteen minute trip on the Sonoma Steam Railroad, a quarter-size reproduction of a mountain division steam railraod of the 1890s, takes you over trestles, past trees, lakes, tunnels and bridges, and into Traintown. While the train takes on water in Lakeville, you can look at this quarter-sized miniature mining town, while listening to its recorded history and feeling like Gulliver in the land of Lilliputians.

The Traintown Express.

JACK LONDON STATE HISTORIC PARK

Glen Ellen. (707) 938-5216. 10-5 daily. $1.50 per car for the museum and the newly enlarged park.

Charmian London built the House of Happy Walls as a memorial to her husband. Furnished with the furniture and art gathered for Wolf House, which burned before the Londons could move into it, this museum thoroughly covers the life of the adventurous young man. Once a sailor, prospector and roustabout, London struggled to gain acceptance as a writer—and you can see a collection of his rejection slips. Photos of the Snark, in which the Londons sailed the South Pacific, and treasures collected on their voyages line the walls. Books sold by the ranger are stamped with London's signature (the stamp he used to save time). London was also an experimental farmer and thirty-nine acres of his Beauty Ranch have just been purchased by the state. Here you'll see the cottage where he did his writing, concrete silos,

the distillery, stallion barn, log bathhouse, and blacksmith's shop. A trail still leads to the Wolf House ruins and to London's grave. Picnic areas are available.

THE WORLD OF JACK LONDON

Jack London Village, 14300 Arnold Drive. Glen Ellen. (707) 996-2888 Wed.–Sun. 10-6 (but there are always 25¢ books on sale on the honor system outside the store.)

Located in a marvelous bookshop specializing in books by Jack London and his friends, this unique museum is a collection of posters made for movies of Jack London's books, plaques, pictures, dishes, memorial cups, letters to and from fans, old checks, Charmian London's typewriter, first editions, scrapbooks, and remembrances. Even the guest book makes good reading!

SONOMA COUNTY FARM TRAILS

P.O. Box 6043, Santa Rosa, CA 95406. For a copy of the map send stamped, self-addressed envelope.

Drive from a mushroom farm and eggery in Petaluma to apple farms in Sebastopol, turkey growers, or Christmas tree farms. The map lists Farm Trail members and has a handy product reference guide. California Christmas Tree Growers are listed at 2855 Telegraph Ave., Berkeley, CA 94705.

SONOMA COUNTY HISTORICAL MUSEUM

557 Summerfield Rd., Santa Rosa (707) 539-0556, 1-5 daily, except Mon. Free.

Old photos of the county and of San Francisco

before and after 1906, a 1902 Sears Roebuck catalog, the Delft plate sent by the Dutch in 1947 as thanks to Santa Rosa's children for three thousand pounds of clothing donated in a war-relief drive, and the first Santa Rosa entry (1966) to the Soap Box Derby are among the many items in this fine collection (scheduled to move to new quarters in the next few months).

RIPLEY'S BELIEVE IT OR NOT MEMORIAL MUSEUM

Juilliard Park, Santa Rosa Ave., Santa Rosa (707) 545-1414, 11-4 daily, until 5 in winter. Adults, 50¢, under 12, 10¢.

Nestled in tall redwoods, this little church, built from *one* tree, houses personal articles and drawings of the Believe-It-or-Not man. A wax figure of Ripley looks out at photos of him with Will Rogers and Shirley Temple, and newspaper clippings as well as samplings of the curiosities he'd collected. You might hear some of the "Believe It or Not" radio shows if the guard has time to play them for you.

Across the street is the *Luther Burbank Memorial Garden* with a kiosk telling the story of his life and showing some of his tools. *Burbank's Home* at Santa Rosa and Sonoma Avenues, is now open Tuesday and Saturday for half hour tours (707) 539-3428. Adults are 50¢, children 10¢ and by appointment). Paderewski played on the piano downstairs; the piano shawl was a gift from Queen Victoria.

JESSE PETER MEMORIAL MUSEUM

Santa Rosa Junior College, 1501 Mendocino Ave., Santa Rosa. (707) 527-4479. 11-4 weekdays, 1-4 Sun. and by appt. Free. Visitor parking behind Bailey Field.

Native American arts are prized in this bustling tiny center. Pottery, drums, crafts, sculpture, a Tule balsa canoe, jars, slide show, and grinding stones are all part of a changing exhibit.

EDWIN LANGHART HEALDSBURG MUSEUM

133 Matheson St., Healdsburg. (707) 433-4717. Tues.– Sat., 1-4, Free.

Treasures from the collections of local families have formed the nucleus of this fine outgrowth of our Bicentennial. Dolls, sewing machines, books, toys, gentlemen's accessories and ladies' clothing, a 1904 washer, an 1892 people-drawn fire engine, a cradle scythe, a funny carved wooden rooster, false teeth and pictures of the geysers are part of this growing display.

CANOE TRIPS ON THE RUSSIAN RIVER

W. C. "Bob" Trowbridge. 20 Healdsburg Ave., Healdsburg, CA 95448. (707) 433-7247.

Nineteen dollars per canoe. Over 5 years old only. Reservations advised. For information on trips on the American River, Feather River, Sacramento River and Colorado River, call or write.

The picturesque, winding Russian River is perfect for family canoe trips. It's safe and lovely but can also be

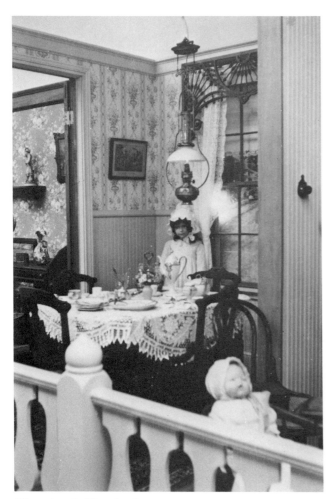
Dinnertime in Victorian Sonoma.

fast enough to be exciting. One-, two-, and half-day trips are available and there's a chicken barbeque on weekends in summer at Windsor Vineyards. Swimmers only!

ITALIAN SWISS COLONY

Hwy. 101, Asti. (707) 894-2541. 9-5 daily. Free.
    "The Little Old Wine Maker" has been replaced by a white-coated scientist amid stainless steel tanks, shiny pipes and chemistry laboratories here at Asti. Junior scientists will enoy this visit, and not just for the free cookies. Picnic facilities are available.

CHARLENE'S YESTERDAYS' MUSEUM

Hwy. 12 out of Sebastopol, Bodega, (707) 876-3282. Wed. –Sun. 11-5, weather and mood permitting. Adults 75¢, children 25¢.
    Hundreds of antique dolls, toys, curiosities, and memories are crammed into a spacious barn. Santa's toy shop, Granma's kitchen and the old schoolhouse look just right. There are French, German and Japanese dolls, Shirley Temple dolls and books, Jeanette MacDonald musical and mechanical dolls, and old-time playthings along with adult-sized versions of Lily Langtry and some of Hollywood's favorites. Picnic in a shady nook and listen to the tapping drums and crashing cymbals of an authentic player piano.

UNION HOTEL RESTAURANT

Occidental. (707) 874-3662. Breakfast on weekends, 7-11, lunch on weekdays 11:30-1:30 ($2.95), Dinner nightly, $5.25-$8.75.

Dining at the Union Hotel, which has been in business since 1867, is more than just a meal, it's an experience: Italian food served family-style on a plastic red-checked tablecloth with more food than you can possibly eat. One lunch consisted of salami & cheese, bean vinaigrette, salad, clam chowder, chicken, zucchini fritters, bread & butter and pasta. Chicken, duck and steak are the evening choices—with salami & cheese, bean salad, thick soup, pickled salad, green salad, sourdough bread and sweet butter, pasta, vegetables, potatoes, side dishes—and dessert. Paper bags for "tomorrow's lunch" come with the check. Everything tastes delicious—especially if you've primed yourself by starving for awhile beforehand.

DUNCAN MILLS DEPOT MUSEUM

Hwy. 116, 4 miles from the ocean. Duncan Mills, (707) 865-2573. 9-5 daily. Free.

The only remaining depot of the North Pacific Coast Railroad, which ran the Sausalito-Cazadero route from 1877 to 1935, is now a small museum of railroad history and the reception office for Duncan Mills Campground. Tools, telegraph keys, bottles, photos, books and various vestiges of the logging railway may be seen. Duncan Mills is a growing outpost, with leather, cheese, book, jewelry and food stores springing up in Victorian style.

Making a wish in Fort Ross.

48

FORT ROSS STATE HISTORIC PARK

Hwy. 1, 12 miles north of Jenner. (707) 847-3286.
10-4:30 daily. $1.50 per car.

Fifty-nine buildings, nine of which are inside the redwood walls of the fort, are being rebuilt in a major state restoration project. The Russian Chapel, with a ringable bell in front, is as spare and quiet as it was when the Fort was sold to John Sutter in 1841. Visitors can climb up into the eight-sided blockade tower and the seven-sided blockade to look out over the little beach and inlet where Russian fur merchants used to trade with the Indians. The Commodore's house serves as a small museum, with a Russian samovar, tools, native plant exhibits, an Aleut kayak, and artifacts found on the grounds. The puppet story of Princess Helene Gagarin's abduction by Chief Solano and her subsequent rescue by General Vallejo, Solano's Blood Brother, is romantic fantasy loosely based on fact. Don't forget to toss a wish into the wishing well!

LAKE COUNTY MUSEUM

Old Courthouse. Main St. Lakeport. (707) 263-2276.
Thur.–Sat., 1-4 in winter, Tues.–Sun. 11-4 in summer.
Free.

Photos of yesteryear—the old spas and steamships—are favorites in this pioneer and Native American collection. An old musket used in the Revolutionary War, a barbed wire collection, a gem collection (Lake County is known for its "moon tears," or semi-precious diamonds), clocks and clothes are here, along with Pomo baskets, feather polychrome baskets, a Tule boat, a rare rabbit blanket, and arrowheads.

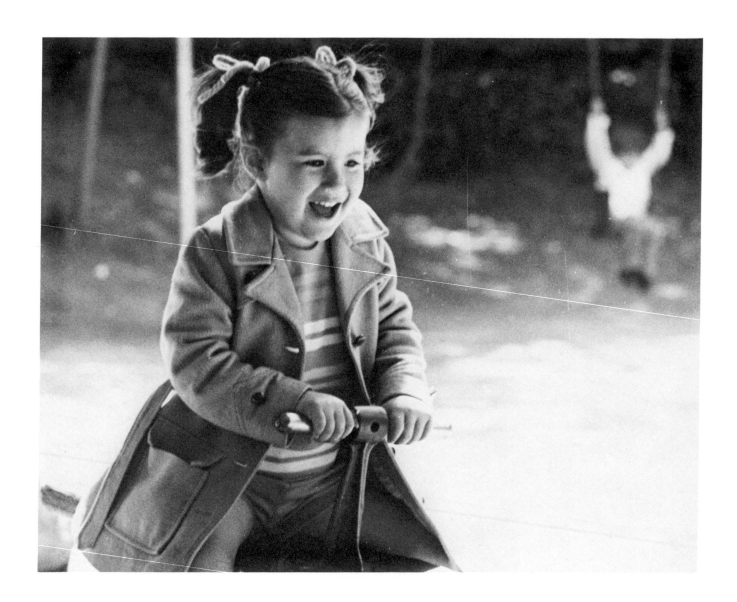

4

REDWOOD COUNTRY: MENDOCINO, HUMBOLDT AND DEL NORTE COUNTIES

Redwood Country is one of the most beautiful areas in America. Stately redwoods line the roads "as far as the fog flows" and the Pacific Ocean crashes into the shoreline. Some of the beaches are craggy and surrounded by dangerous currents. Others are calm and protected, with long empty stretches just made for solitary walks. You can dash up from San Francisco on Hwy. 101 or you can spend hours wending along the coastline on Hwy. 1. You can enjoy the Victoriana of Ferndale and Eureka or you can lose yourself in the tiny fishing villages of Rockport and Noyo. Whale watching is a popular pastime. The waters may be too cold to swim in, but the fish thrive, and are there for the catching. You can get away from it all in the sylvan glens and picnic areas along the Avenue of the Giants, marveling on man's smallness next to a three hundred foot tree. Redwood Country lets you set your own pace—there are many places to see and things to do close to each other, and there are enough parks and beaches for you to relax or picnic in, whenever the mood strikes. It's a perfect place for a weekend, or a week.

MENDOCINO

Once an old lumber port, settled in 1852, Mendocino is now a mecca for driftwood collectors and artists. The town has appeared in many movies and there are interesting little streets to browse along when it gets too foggy for beachcombing. Among the highlights in town are *The Mendocino Art Center (540 Little Lake St. 10-5 daily, special movies and shows at night, (707) 937-5819), The Mendocino Ice Cream Company* on Main (937-5844), *Sky's No Limit*, the kite and frisbee store on Main (937-0173) and *Kolorphorme*, the toy store for all ages down the block (937-0100). The old *Masonic Lodge Hall*, at Lansing and Ukiah, with its massive redwood sculpture of Father Time And The Maiden, carved from one piece of redwood, is a landmark, and the *Kelly House Historical Museum*, on Main, is currently being restored (957-5791, Fri. — Tues. and by appointment. Free.) to its 1861 state and will be a memory-filled museum.

MASONITE CORP. DEMONSTRATION FOREST

Hwy. 128 between Navarro and Little River.
This six hundred-yard forest trail shows a commercially grown forest. Points of interest are well-marked. A display of how masonite is made from log leftovers, to chips, to fiber, to blank board, to pressed board, to panels and finally used is available, as is a nice picnic area.

GEORGIA PACIFIC LOGGING MUSEUM

90 W. Redwood, Ft. Bragg. (707) 964-5651. Mon. –Fri., 8-5. Free.
Built in 1857 as the guesthouse for the Indian reservation army post, this small white house is now surrounded by huge, awe-inspiring machines that were used in the 1880s for hauling logs out of the forest and for skidding them onto the landing. A huge slice of redwood that was 1,753 years old in 1843 is also on display. Inside, historical pictures of the industry, huge bellows, mementos of the loggers, and ship's models complete the museum collection, which will be moved soon to the large redwood mansion on Main Street, diagonally across from the Skunk Depot. Occasional films help accentuate the differences between the smooth industrial present and the rugged past in logging. Nearby, at the foot of Walnut St., is the *Georgia Pacific Nursery (9-4 weekdays, April-Nov.)* which holds four million trees. A display room explains reforestation and timber management. An arboretum, nature trails, and picnic tables are available. A free packet of redwood seeds is mailed to each visiting family.

MENDOCINO COAST BOTANICAL GARDENS

18220 No. Hwy. 1, 2 mi. south of Ft. Bragg. (707) 964-4352. Adults, $2.50, ages 13-18, $1.50. 9-6 daily in summer, weekends, weather permitting, in winter.
Whole families of quail live in this flower-laden, 47-acre forest and sea coast garden. Visitors walk through nurseries, beside twinkling brooks, over wooden bridges and out to the very edge of the ocean. A cliff-house overlooks the sea-swept rocks. Picnic areas are available, as is a coffee gallery and nursery.

THE SKUNK RAILROAD

Skunk Depot, Ft. Bragg. (707) 964-6371. Reservations advised (write: Calif. Western Railroad, P.O. Box 907, Ft. Bragg 95437). Half- and full-day trips from and to Fort Bragg and Willits to Northspur are available at prices ranging from about $4 for children for a 3-hour trip to about $10 for adults for the full day.
The Skunk Railroad, named for the smell the first gas engines used to cast over the countryside, has been making passenger trips from Ft. Bragg to Willits since

1911. During the forty-mile trip the train crosses thirty-two trestles and bridges, goes through two tunnels, twists and turns over spectacularly curved track and travels from quiet Noyo riverbed to high mountain passes through redwood forest. The bouncy diesel Skunk and roaring Steam Super Skunk are both well worth the price and time. One train even has an open observation car.

WELLER HOUSE

524 Stewart, Ft. Bragg (707) 964-3061, 10-5 p.m. daily in summer, weekends in winter and by appointment. $1.25 for adults, children under 12, 50¢.

Built in 1886 by Horace Weller, one of Ft. Bragg's leading citizens, this national historic landmark boasts a breathtaking redwood ballroom on the top floor. The new owners, Andre and Arlene Schade, enjoy showing young visitors the pictures of the Weller family, their own 1929 toy train and dolls, the ship models, many pianos and harpsichords, and old gramaphone. Mr. Schade even has his own teddy bear and his grandmother's German doll—and a table crafted by Charles Eastlake.

MENDOCINO COUNTY MUSEUM

400 E. Commercial St., Willits (707) 459-2736. 10-4:30, Wed.–Sun. Ages 19-64, 75¢; 11-18, 50¢; 65 and over, 25¢.

Historical articles and documents reflecting Mendocino County's past have been gathered for this interesting collection that includes a peddler's wagon, stage coaches, a lumber room, restored kitchen, living and bedrooms, Pomo baskets and a wonderful assortment of hats. If the Skunk Railroad leaves you in Willits with time to spend, this museum is a nice way to do it.

THE DRIVE-THRU TREE

Hwy. 1, Leggett. (707) 925-6363. Daily, 9-6, later in summer. $2 per car.

This large, chandelier-shaped, 315-foot redwood was tunneled in 1934 and a standard-size contemporary car just fits through. It's twenty-one feet in diameter and —in spite of the tunnel—is still alive. The winding dirt road leading to the tree takes you right to a little gift shop and on to the highway. There are two hundred acres of nature trails and picnic areas by the side of a lake that is home to geese. Logging relics are on the grounds.

REDWOOD DEMONSTRATION FORESTS

To show the diverse aims, methods and benefits of industrial forest management within the redwood region, several firms have made demonstration forests available to the public. Tours are self-guided and there are rest rooms and picnic areas available. You'll learn that only 1 percent of the tree is living—only the tips of its roots, the leaves, buds, flowers, seed, and a single thin layer of cells sheathing the tree. You see Douglas firs, white firs and redwood residuals—the redwood trees that have sprung up from seeds and sprouts in three generations. Seven separate installations each tell the same story in a little different way:

Masonite Corporation's demonstration forest is just west of Navarro on Highway 128. One mile north of

Rockport on Hwy. 1, the *Louisiana Pacific Corporation* provides a four-hundred-yard, twenty-minute walk along a scenic creek. Visit the *Pacific Lumber Company* four miles south of Scotia on Hwy. 101 and the *Simpson Timber Company*, one mile east of Blue Lake on Hwy. 299 to Redding. The *Samoa Division* of the Louisiana-Pacific Corp. is one mile north of Trinidad on *old* Hwy. 101.

Three miles south of Crescent City on Hwy. 101, the Rellim Redwood Co. provides an excellent demonstration forest tour guide, showing logging history, reforestation, and identification drawings of the plants you'll see amid the redwoods.

CONFUSION HILL

Hwy. 101, Piercy. (707) 925-6546. 8:30-7:30 daily, April-Sept. Confusion Mysteries: Adults, $1.50, ages 6-12, 75¢. Mountain train: Adults, $1.50, ages 6-12, 75¢.

The miniature Mountain Train follows many switchbacks to take you one-and-one-quarter miles up to the summit of a redwood mountain, through a tunnel tree, and back down. Back at the bottom of the mountain, try the other experience at Confusion Hill—a spot where gravity is defied and your eyes tell lies. You seem to be standing sideways; water runs uphill; your friends shrink or grow taller in front of you. Be sure to check out the Redwood Shoe and the 250-foot tree house. Nobody knows why all of this happens, but the kids are delighted by it.

PAT DERBY'S FAMOUS WILD ANIMALS (HOWLING WOLF LODGE)

Hwy. 101, Leggett. (707) 925-6211. 9 a.m. to dusk, daily.

Pat Derby and Sweet William

54

MENDOCINO, HUMBOLDT AND DEL NORTE COUNTIES

Adults, $1, children under 12, 50ᶜ.

Sweet William, black bear star of "Gentle Ben"; Stanley Goodwolf; Spot, a leopard that worked on "Daktari"; Christopher, the Mercury cougar; Ricochet, the Mercury bobcat; Harriet the Baboon and other animals are put through their paces here by their glamorous trainer, Pat Derby. All of the animals are tv, movie, and commercial stars and you may even see some of them in action before the cameras during your visit. Rooms to rent and a small restaurant are also on the premises.

AVENUE OF THE GIANTS

Humboldt Redwoods State Park, Weott. (707) 946-2311.

Standing tall as a nominee for most spectacular thirty-three miles anywhere, is this bypass road winding leisurely beneath three-hundred-foot trees. One of the few tree species to have survived from the time of the dinosaurs, the redwoods are awesome, majestic trees to behold. You'll drive through a protected wilderness of massive, soaring trees and moss and fern carpeted landscape occasionally spotted with deer. Founder's Grove, Rockefeller Forest and Children's Forest are some of the best of the special groves. *The Tree House* in Piercy, *Hobbiton* and the *Chimney Tree* near Phillipsville, and the *Drive-Thru Tree* in Myers Flat are more commercial stopping places.

PACIFIC LUMBER COMPANY

Scotia, 27 miles south of Eureka. (707) 764-2222. Free museum and mill tours in summer, Mon.–Fri., 10-4.

Scotia is an old logging town that was built entirely

of redwood. The museum, a fine old mansion, presents pictures of the loggers at work and play and a collection of logging equipment, tools and relics. Here's where you get the pass for the self-guided tour of the mill, which takes about forty-five minutes and follows the processing of a log from the moment it comes off the truck. The first step is one of the most impressive—a debarker that uses water pressure to peel the log as if it were a banana. Many things go on all at once in the mill (which can be loud and more scary for timid mothers than for the kids). The nearby *Scotia Fish Rearing Pond*, built by the lumber company to help rehabilitate the Eel River, raises 100,000 steelhead and salmon each year.

ALTON & PACIFIC RAILROAD

Hwy. 36, one-half mile east of Hwy. 101, Alton. (Rte. 1, Box 477, Fortuna 95540. No phone). Thurs.–Tues., 11-5, Memorial Day through Labor Day. Adults $2, ages 3-15, $1.25.

The Alton & Pacific Railroad is the only two-foot narrow gauge, wood-burning steam train on the West Coast and a ride on this rattling relic is a must for train buffs of any age. Minimum trip: at least four fares.

DEPOT MUSEUM

Park St., Fortuna. (707) 725-2495, 12-5, daily in summer. Closed Thursday and Fridays, Sept.-May. Donation.

The 1893 train depot is now a small museum housing Fortuna memories of the loggers, the farmers, the Indians and the railroad. The old teletyper is at the ready; fancy dresses and shoes wait for the next dance; fishing

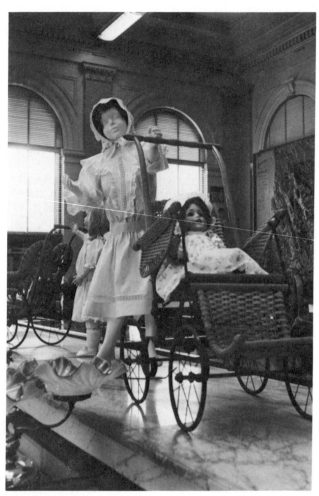

Out for a stroll in Old Town.

poles and tackle stand waiting for the next fishing trip and pictures and school books round out the collection. The three old marriage certificates are lovely. Visitors in the Autumn may want to stop by *Clendenen's Cider Works (Twelfth St. and Newberg Rd., 725-2133)* to see the mill in action and buy fresh cider. *The Dollhouse Museum* at 1710 Main St. (725-3738, 9-6 daily; adults 50¢, children 25¢) houses a remarkable collection of old and rare dollhouses and dollhouse furnishings including a mouse house (with seashell beds), an 1880 German castle, a 1920 kitchen and "The Old Lady Who Lived in a Shoe." *Chapman's Gem and Mineral Shop and Museum*, four miles south of the city on Hwy. 101 (725-4732) is open in summer, 10-5 daily.

FERNDALE MUSEUM

Shaw and 3rd Sts., Ferndale (707) 786-4222 for info. Tues.—Sun. 1-4. Donation.

The Portuguese, Swiss, Danish, and English founding families of this Victorian village are celebrated in this still-to-be completed historical museum. The Lytels and Shaws have also donated memorabilia—including photographs and clothes. A walk along Main Street, with stops at Geppetto's Book and Toy Store and Sweetness and Light, a real old-fashioned candy store, is also fun.

CLARKE MEMORIAL MUSEUM

Third and E Streets, Eureka. (707) 443-1947, Tues.—Sat., 10-4. Free.

This large pioneer museum has had a major overhaul. Located in a 1912 bank, changing exhibits are

56

presented in airy, attractive new settings. Indian baskets, gun collections, ships' bells, old typewriters, sewing machines, and antique dolls are displayed among mementos of early Humboldt County life, the maritime days, and from the Pomo Indians. The Clarke Memorial Museum is located in Eureka's *Old Town*, a restored section of town on the waterfront of Humboldt Bay. The commercial and residential Victorian buildings, crowned by the most photographed building in the west, the Carson Mansion (at Second and M) includes shops, boutiques, a gift shop in a railroad car, the *Bon Boniere Ice Cream Parlor* at 215 F, *Windjammer Books*, and the *Angelus* (420 2nd) which specializes in music boxes and old dolls. If you want to see how oysters are processed, stop by at *The Coast Oyster Co.* at the foot of A St. (9-2 Mon.—Fri. in winter, 442-2947) for a self-guided tour, then taste them next door at Lazio's Restaurant.

THE M/V MADAKET BAY TOUR

Sails from the foot of C Street, Eureka. 1, 2:30 and 4 p.m. in summer. (707) 442-3738. Adults, $3; ages 12-17, $2; 6-11, $1.50.

The seventy-five minute cruise aboard this venerable vessel takes in the oyster beds, pelican roosts, saw mills, egret rookery, former Indian village, and history of the area. An adults-only cocktail cruise sails at 5:30 on weekends.

SEQUOIA PARK & ZOO

Glatt and W Streets. (707) 443-7331, 10-7 daily in summer, til 5 in winter. Closed on holidays. Free.

One hundred-fifty kinds of animals, mostly native to the area, are housed in this beautiful new zoo, the only one in the world in a redwood setting. There are river otters, Big Horn sheep, llamas, sitka deer, bear, birds, and chimpanzees and there's also a petting zoo for children. Playgrounds and picnic areas are available in the park.

FORT HUMBOLDT SHP

3431 Fort Ave., off Hwy. 101, Eureka. (707) 433-4588/ 443-7952. 9-6 daily. Free.

High on a windy hill overlooking a modern logging facility, Fort Humboldt is primarily an outdoor museum of the logging industry. Old machinery is accompanied by large billboards telling what it was like to be a logger in the nineteenth century. A logger's cabin is furnished with a stove, a bed, a shelf of beans and a "pin-up" calendar. You learn how to "fall" a tree (the falling branches are called "widow makers"), then see how to drag it out of the forest and cut it up. One logger notes that it's "a shame to wash clothes while they can still bend." An 1884 Falk locomotive and an 1892 Andersonia locomotive are on view. Old Fort Humboldt, where U. S. Grant served as a staff officer in the 1850s, is nearby. A short film on the steam age of logging is shown regularly. A short drive away are the only two *Covered Bridges* in the area. Take 101 South to Elk River Road and follow along to either Zane or Bertas Road. They're covered not to protect them from snow, but to protect the lumber from rain—boarding them up preserves the wood longer and is less expensive than constant repainting.

SAMOA COOKHOUSE

Samoa Road, Eureka. (707) 442-1659. Breakfast: 7-11, adults $2.95, ages 7-11, $1.95, 3-6, $1.10. Lunch: 11-2, adults $2.85, ages 7-11, $1.85; 3-6, $1.05. Dinner: 5-10, adults $5.75, ages 7-11, $3.25, 3-6, $1.95.

Family-style meals are served seven days a week in this old lumbercamp cookhouse which once served as relief quarters for shipwreck victims. The long tables are set as they were in 1900 with red-and-white checked cloths and large bottles of catsup. Our breakfast consisted of huge amounts of orange juice, coffee, delicious French toast, and made-by-hand sausages. Dinner the night before included thick cuts of ham and sole, and peach pie with all the fixings. Before or after the meal, wander through the adjoining rooms to see an assemblage of logger's boots, dinner bells, kitchen utensils, and a steam coffeemaker that once served five hundred men three times a day.

HUMBOLDT STATE UNIVERSITY MARINE LABORATORY

Trinidad. (707) 677-3671 Mon.–Fri., 8-5; Sat. and Sun. 12-5 during the school year. Free.

Located at Land's End, in the picturesque fishing village of Trinidad, this working laboratory is open to the public for self-guided tours. Hallway aquariums hold rare and common molluscs and crustaceans, and fresh- and salt-water fish. Vari-colored anemones, wall-eye surf perches, Siamese Tiger fish and shovel-nose catfish were there for our visit, along with a wolf eel that has been tamed and a small black octopus.

Do stop at the *Trinidad Lighthouse* on your way to the lab. This is the spot where the Spaniards landed on Trinity Sunday in 1775. The original gear system of descending weights still works to turn the light, but the original two-ton bell is for display only.

Patrick's Point State Park along the shore north of the laboratory boasts a small museum of Yurok artifacts and rock displays at park headquarters. (707) 677-3570. There is an admission for each car.

PRAIRIE CREEK REDWOODS STATE PARK

Hwy. 101, near Orick. (707) 488-2861. 9-5 daily. Free.

Roosevelt elk roam this state park and can usually be seen grazing across the meadow from the Visitors Center. A small but interesting exhibit on the elk and the trees, ferns, flowers and animals of the area is on display. The most extraordinary object is a madrone tree that grew to envelope the skull of an elk.

Just south of the park, on 101, is the *Prairie Creek Fish Hatchery (488-2253, 8-5 daily, free)* which raises King and Silver salmon and Coastal Cut-throat and Rainbow trout.

Just north of Orick, at Bald Hills Road junction, the *Arcata Redwood Company's Mill "A,"* welcomes visitors to view operations from overhead catwalks. A Forest Renewal Exhibit is five miles farther north.

KLAMATH JET BOAT KRUISES

Hwy. 101, 1 mile north of Klamath. (707) 482-4191. Leaves at 9 a.m.; returns at 3. $12.50 for adults. Ages 4-11, $5. Group rates available. Reservations advisable.

Skimming over the Klamath River on a jet-boat is

an exciting experience. Deer, raccoon, bear, and other animals are often spotted on the riverbank, and the rock formations alongside the river make this sixty-four mile trip truly memorable. Hoopa Indians can be seen living with their age-old ways when lunch is taken at the Klamath Lodge where local Indian handiwork is on display (or, if you prefer, bring your own picnic).

TREES OF MYSTERY

Hwy. 101, Klamath. (707) 482-5613. 7:30 a.m.–7:30 p.m. Mon.–Fri.; until 10 p.m. in summer, 8-5 daily in winter. Closed holidays. Adults $3.50; ages 6-12 $1.75.

A talking forty-nine-foot Paul Bunyan greets you at the entrance, and then you walk through a hollowed redwood log into a forest of redwoods, where recorded music and explanations take you past trees such as "The Fallen Giant," and "The Elephant Tree," and the immense and moving "Cathedral Tree." Going back down the hill is our favorite section—Paul Bunyan's "Trail of Tall Tales," where you hear how Babe the Blue Ox was found, how the Grand Canyon was dug, and how Sourdough Sam makes his pancakes (his recipe includes the lard from one summer-fatted bear). The "End of the Trail" museum in the gift shop offers an array of baskets, clothes and artifacts of tribes ranging from the Mississippi to the Pacific and north to the Aleutians.

The *Tour-Thru Tree* on 101 at the north end of the Klamath River Bridge (known for its decorative golden bears) may be worth a short visit.

Welcome to the Land of the Blue Ox.

UNDERSEA GARDENS

Anchor Way, Cresent City. (707) 464-3522. July and Aug., 9:30-5:45, daily. June and Sept., 10-5. Adults $2.50; 12-18 $1.75; 6-12 $1.50. Family group $8.50.

Dive show every hour on the hour from 10 to 5. Over five thousand marine specimens live in this habitat ten feet below sea level. The ferocious wolf eels, scurrying crabs, sun starfish, and black snappers that stand vertically to aid their digestion are all native to the area and presented in their normal environments. A skin diver regularly gives underwater demonstrations showing how Armstrong, the octopus, moves and sea anemones eat. You'll see sables, big skates and dogfish sharks as well as Stanley, the Sturgeon, and starry flounders, too.

DEL NORTE HISTORICAL SOCIETY MUSEUM

577 H Street, Crescent City (707) 464-3922. Tues.–Sat. 10-12 and 1-4:30. Free.

The 1935 version of "Last of the Mohicans" was filmed in Crescent City and this museum, once the county jail, has many photos of the Indians who appeared in it. A Yurok bark house and stick games, headdresses, beads, dolls and baskets of the Tolowa, Pomo, Hoopa and Yurok tribes are shown, as are photos of Crescent City since its beginnings, with lots of "before and after" shots of the 1964 tidal wave. Unicycles, an early steam donkey used in logging, jail cells, local craftsmen's tools (including a moonshine still), pioneer clothing and other collections by local residents will occupy your time here.

Down the block, at 710 H Street, is the *McNulty*

Pioneer Memorial Home (464-3922, Tues.–Sat., 1-4. Free), a charming nineteenth century redwood house built as a wedding present. A handsome carved bedroom set and baby's cradle with dolls, a bass mandolin piano and a sewing machine give the house a lived-in look. We were especially impressed with a carved rosewood sixteenth century Italian chair and the picture of Victor, a red setter. Victor's mistress used to send him to the store with money and a shopping list in a basket and he would carry the groceries home to her.

BATTERY POINT LIGHTHOUSE

Crescent City. Wed.–Sun. 9-5, at low tide. Free.

Battery Point Lighthouse is located offshore from Crescent City on a little island accessible only at low tide. The original light is still workable and the old log book, banjo clock, shipwreck photos and nautical mementos add to the enjoyment of a visit. Although most children have hopes of being stranded by the tide, the wealth of native plants and view of the ocean from the tower will make up for their disappointment in finding themselves safely back on the Mainland.

SHIP ASHORE

Smith River. (707) 487-3141. April-Dec. 9 a.m.-8 p.m. Free.

This 160-foot former luxury yacht, which also served with the U.S. Navy during World War II, is now a land-locked gift shop with a complete naval and historical museum under the main deck. The wheel house is full of ship models—from a seventeenth century Man O'War to a World War II vessel—and kids can take a turn at the wheel itself. An autograph and the address of Nukuo Fujita, the only Japanese pilot to drop a firebomb on the United States, is on the wall. Downstairs you'll find a potpourri of memories and souvenirs that range from a 1910 country doctor's kit to Alaskan boots, stuffed owls and armadillos, an extensive shell collection, ship blueprints, swords and uniforms, clothes and necklaces from the Edward Lopez family of the Tolowa tribe, and a fascinating pirate's den that gives lore and rules pirates lived by.

PUBLIC RELATIONS TOURS

CROWN SIMPSON PULP COMPANY. Fairhaven. (707) 443-9771. Free tours, by reservation, for those over 8, Mon.—Fri. at 1 p.m., Memorial Day to Sept. 1. A half-hour tour shows how huge piles of woodchips are ground into pulp, and a fifteen minute slide show explains what you've seen.

SIMPSON KORBEL FOREST NURSERY. Hwy. 299 near Blue Lake in Korbel. (707) 822-0371. Free tours, daily, 11 a.m. and 1 p.m. in summer.

MAD RIVER STATE FISH HATCHERY. Blue Lake. (707) 822-0592. 8-5 daily. Free. Salmon and steelhead fish eggs, baby fish and fingerlings may be seen by the drop-in visitor. By the way, the river is not ferocious. It was named for a fight between Joe Greeg and L. K. Wood, two explorers of the region, in 1849.

RUMIANO CHEESE CO. Ninth and E Streets. Crescent City. (707) 464-4623. Mon.—Sat. at 9 a.m. in summer and by appointment. Visitors can see a third generation of cheesemakers producing huge wheels of dry jack cheese, as well as Monterey and pepper jack (and other flavors, depending on the day).

PAUL'S SALMON CANNERY. On the west side of Hwy. 101, one-half mile north of Klamath. (707) 482-4591. Tours by appointment, in season from June-Sept.

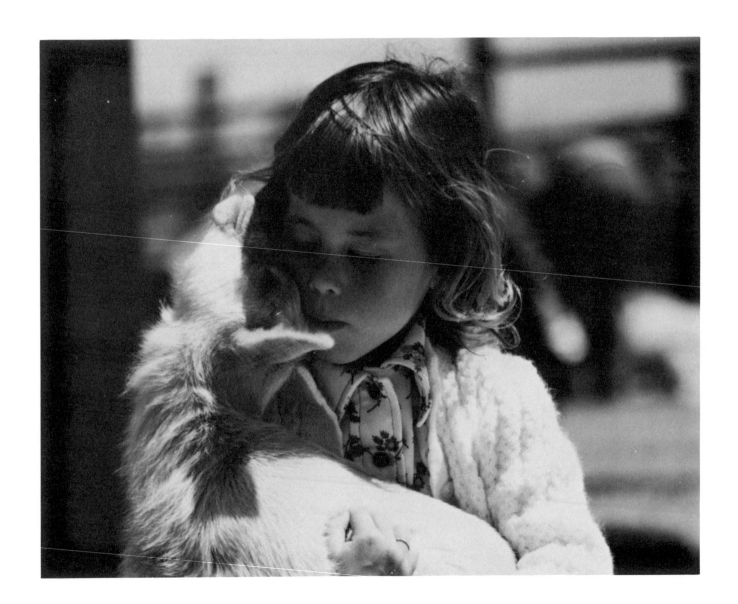

5

THE PENINSULA AND
THE SAN JOSE AREA

The Peninsula and the San Jose area can provide many days of happy "attraction" hunting. There are huge amusement parks—such as Frontierland and Marriott's Great America—small museums, lovely parks, and interesting industries. A map showing city streets is helpful, and it might be a good idea to plan your day before you set out. Fast foods flourish on all of the roads here, and picnic areas are always close by, so impromptu meals are easy.

SANCHEZ ADOBE

Linda Mar Blvd., Pacifica. (415) 359-1881. Tues. and Sun. 1-5 and by appt. (574-6441). Free.
    As the center of the Mission Dolores rancho and the site of the earliest Spanish settlement in San Mateo County, the Sanchez Adobe has lived through four periods of history which will soon be reflected in the buildings and restorations now in progress. Artifacts from the aboriginal Indians were discovered during an archaeological dig in 1978 and the San Mateo Historical Society hopes to put together an Indian village. The farmlands once produced the food for San Francisco's Mission Dolores and the mission outpost is now outlined on the adobe grounds. In 1842, Sr. Sanchez, who served as the *alcalde*, or mayor, of San Francisco built his home here. The adobe still stands and is filled with his rancho mementos (especially in the tackroom/workroom downstairs) and the Victorian furniture and clothes of Sanchez's children and grandchildren.

COYOTE POINT MUSEUM

Coyote Point Park, San Mateo. (415) 573-2595. Tues.–Fri. 9-6; weekends 1-5. Free. $2 per car for park use.

This small, nicely arranged museum covers all aspects of the natural history of San Mateo. Creatures native to the area, bayshore birds, shells, fossils, and dioramas of chaparral and redwood wildlife are featured. Our troop was most fascinated by the skeleton of a horse and the exhibit on natural camouflage in birds and butterflies. The picnic grounds nearby are always breezy.

JAPANESE TEA GARDEN

Central Park, San Mateo. (415) 574-6975. Mon.–Fri. 9-4; weekends, 11-5. Free.

This proper, gracious Japanese garden is a soothing spot in the midst of city bustle. Quaint bridges and rock pathways take the visitor past a waterfall, a pond thick with waterlilies and goldfish and, in the springtime, delicate cherry blossoms. The teahouse is open, irregularly, in summer.

SAN MATEO COUNTY HISTORICAL MUSEUM

1700 W. Hillsdale Blvd. College of San Mateo, San Mateo. (415) 574-6441. Mon.–Fri. 9:30-4:30; Sat., 10:30-4:30; Sun., 12-4. Free.

A walk through this museum is a walk through history. You begin with the Pleistocene period—14 million years ago—and view bones and fossils found in San Mateo from that age. Then on to the Costanoan Indians of 3,000 years ago, and the description of their

Searching for golden carp in San Jose.

magic dances, boats, tools, and food. The Mission Rancho period is well-represented and exhibits of lumber mills, an old general store and bar, settlers' wagons and unicycles speak for the pioneers. An 1860s kitchen and 1880 Victorian living room are being designed.

FARRELL'S ICE CREAM PARLOUR

109 Bovet Rd., San Mateo. (415) 345-1894. Sun.–Thurs. 11:30-11, Fri. and Sat. until 12:30.

Farrell's brings all of a child's fantasies to life in its birthday extravaganzas. Drums pound, whistles and bells blow, candles are lit, and the entire restaurant sings to the birthday child. The birthday party Zoo sundae of eight ice creams, five sherbets, five toppings, almonds, whipped cream, cherries and bananas goes for $12.50 and comes with at least ten spoons. Other Farrell's favorites start at 80¢ for an old-fashioned soda, shake or sundae (soda water is still 2¢ plain) and end with the Pig's Trough. There's a special award if you finish this one by yourself. Sandwiches of all kinds are available, too.

There are other Farrell's in Sunnyvale, Fremont, Sacramento, Hayward, Fresno, and Daly City's Serramonte Shopping Center.

MARINE WORLD/AFRICA USA

Marine World Parkway off Bayshore Freeway, Redwood City. (415) 365-7446/D-O-L-P-H-I-N. 9:30-6 daily in summer, closed Mon. and Tues. during spring and fall; open weekends only in winter. $7.50 adults, $4.50 ages 5-12 covers all shows.

Marine World/Africa USA is, as advertised, really wild. Although the price may seem high, you'll find that the family can spend the entire day there happily and not pay for anything else except food, which you can pack along. Shows are scheduled so you can go from one to another at an easy pace. You can watch trained whales and jungle cats, cheer the Dolphin Olympics, take a river raft, pet a porpoise or an aoudad, wander through a fun-filled jungle, and see water-ski shows and puppet shows.

MARINE ECOLOGICAL INSTITUTE

811 Harbor Blvd., Redwood City (415) 364-2760.

Tours aboard the eighty-five-foot research vessel *Inland Seas* offer introduction to the delicate ecology of San Francisco Bay and the Delta. Instructors point out marsh and marine life, discuss currents and waves, pollution, land fill, and planning. Half-day, day, and five-day cruises, and shore field trips are available.

FILOLI HOUSE AND GARDEN

Canada Road, Woodside. (415) 366-4640. Tues.–Fri. at 10 and 1; Sat. at 10 and by appointment. Adults $3 garden, $5 house and garden; children, $3.

If you'd like to walk through the gardens that starred in "Heaven Can Wait," here's your chance. You can also walk through the first floor of this forty-three-room Stuart-style mansion, the former estate of Mrs. William P. Roth. Tours take two hours and are by reservation only.

WEST BAY MODEL RAILROAD CLUB

1090 Merrill St., Menlo Park. (415) 323-3898. Third Fri. and fourth Wed. of each month, 8-10 p.m. Free.

Three different-sized trains run on the club's four thousand feet of track, whistling past miniature towns and painted scenery and over tiny bridges and turntables. Adding to the effectiveness of the show is a tape of special sound effects interspersed with the story of how the club came about. The club also has a railroad-stationary display, a library and a machine shop. The members' special Christmas show on a December weekend is a favorite event for local youngsters.

STANFORD UNIVERSITY

Stanford Campus. (415) 497-2300. Stanford Guide Service, Hoover Institute Lobby, 497-2053. Mon.–Fri. 8-5; Sat. 8:30-1, Sun., 10-4. Stanford Linear Accelerator Center by appointment, 854-3300 ext. 2204.

Hoover Institution on War, Revolution and Peace (497-2053, Mon.–Fri. 8-5, Free. Observatory Platform, 25¢, weekdays 11-12 and 1-4; Sat., 10-12 and 1-4; Sun., 1-4.) In addition to the lovely view from the tower, the Hoover Institute offers memories of Herbert Hoover and his White House years and world crusades. A settee and chairs that belonged to Abraham Lincoln are also on view. *Leland Stanford, Jr., Museum (497-4177, Tues.–Fri. 10-4:45; weekends 1-4:45. Free)* Remembrances of the Stanford family are displayed in this luxurious building, along with a widely varied collection of Indian artifacts, European and primitive art and sculpture, a jade collection, and an Egyptorium, with a mummy in an open case. The Stanford Rooms feature toy trains and soldiers, a check signed by George Washington, children's books, weapons, archaeological findings from Pompeii, and Mrs. Stanford's gowns. The original "Gold Spike," driven in 1869 to complete the nation's first transcontinental railroad is in a special case.

BAYLANDS NATURE INTERPRETIVE CENTER

2775 Embarcadero Road, Palo Alto. (415) 329-2506. Wed.–Fri. 2-5; weekends 10-12, 1-5. Free.

This bayside nature center is on the pilings out in a salt marsh, handy for the nature walks and ecology workshops it excels in. The exhibits show local birds, plants, and a salt-water aquarium. On weekends, there are nature movies and slide lectures, as well as talks and demonstrations.

PALO ALTO JUNIOR MUSEUM AND ZOO

Rinconada Park, 1451 Middlefield Road, Palo Alto. (415) 329-2111. Tues.–Fri., 10-12, 1-5; Sat. 10-5; Sun. and holidays, 1-4. Free.

This beautifully constructed museum has constantly changing exhibits to keep kids coming back for more. The permanent collection includes a large camera obscura, fossils, nests, and Native American artifacts. Outside, in the poured concrete shelters, there are snakes and reptiles, bobcats, ravens, squirrels and lovable rabbits. Ducks nest under the bridge that curves over the pretty pond.

MARRIOTT'S GREAT AMERICA

No. 1 Great American Parkway, off Bayshore Freeway, Santa Clara. (415) 988-1800. Wed.–Mon. 10-9 in summer (until 10 on some summer weekends); weekends only in spring and fall. $9.75, Adults; $8.75 ages 4-11. Seniors, $7.50.

The entrance fee covers every ride, every amusement, and every show—more than enough to keep you hopping for an entire day. There are one hundred rides, from the double-decker carousel to the chilling Tidal Wave, to the Turn of the Century, as well as the world's largest motion picture screen, the Bugs Bunny Wonder Circus, Fort Fun, and live shows. Families amble through theme areas of shops and restaurants such as Orleans Place and Yankee Harbor, a nineteenth century New England Fishing Village. And along with the expected appetite-tempters you can even buy Bugs Bunny carrots of mammoth size, with the greens still attached.

FOOTHILL COLLEGE ELECTRONICS MUSEUM

12345 El Monte Road, Foothill College, Los Altos Hills. (415) 948-8590 x381. Wed. and Thurs., 9-5; Fri. 9-8; Sat. and Sun. 1-5, when school is in session. Free.

The most complete collection of ancient radio tubes, spark transmitters and klytrons in the world is now open to radio hobbyists of all ages. Special exhibits that allow visitors to experiment with tubes, transmitters and receivers are most popular. At this writing, the Foothill College Space Science Center and Planetarium was closed because of Proposition 13. It's right across the street from the Electronics Museum, so do check to see if it's open again.

ENGINE HOUSE

672 Alberta, near Hollenbach and Fremont, Sunnyvale. (415) 245-0609. Wed.–Fri., 12-5; Sat. 10-5; Sun. 12-5; longer hours in summer and just before Christmas.

One million items ("the next million we have on order") of interest to train fans are crammed into this treasure-filled space. Cars, kits, photos, hobby magazines, models of trains from old wood-burners to BART, and everything you'd need to create a complete train world can be found in this, the largest train shop in the west.

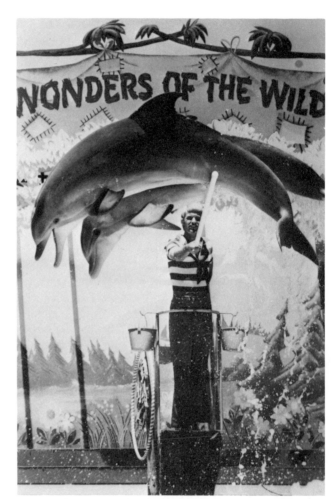

Nimo and Neptune go through their paces.

67

Nearby, the *Sunnyvale Historical Museum* (235 E. California Ave., 739-3642) is open daily, except Wednesday and is free.

MINOLTA PLANETARIUM

De Anza College. 21250 Stevens Creek Blvd. and Stelling Road, Cupertino. Special changing shows on Tuesday and Thursday through Sunday, with different prices. (408) 996-4814.

The Minolta Planetarium employs the latest audio-visual equipment and techniques to present remarkable shows. The main projector spreads the night sky across a fifty-foot dome, and twenty-four sound speakers and one hundred fifty other projectors are used to produce some dazzling effects. These mechanical marvels take you not only through space but through time; you fly to the moon to look at the brilliance of the stars, as they were seen by the astronauts, then you travel back in time to see how the stars looked to man when he first saw them. It's a wondrous experience that combines education and entertainment.

The new *Environmental Studies Area*, open 12-4 on the first Saturday of each month and by appointment, provides a variety of biological environments representing major communities in California.

Le Petit Trianon Museum (996-4712) features rotating exhibits on California history.

HAKONE JAPANESE GARDENS

21000 Big Basin Way, Saratoga. (408) 867-3438 x 50. Daily, 10-5; closed holidays. Teahouse open in summer.

Walk along curving foliage-lined paths, through a wisteria-covered arbor, step on three stones to get across a stream next to three waterfalls. Climb a moon bridge to see the goldfish. Discover little houses and gazebos hidden in the trees. Spy stone and wooden lanterns, statutes of cranes and cats hidden in the foliage. Rest in a peaceful, tatami-matted teahouse overlooking shaped trees. Sit in a wisteria-roofed summerhouse. This wonderful garden was designed by a former court gardener to the Emperor of Japan as a hill and water garden, the strolling pond style typical of Zen gardens in the seventeenth century.

The *SARATOGA HISTORICAL PARK AND MUSEUM* (20450 S. Saratoga-Los Gatos Road, Saratoga, 867-4311) is just getting organized.

VILLA MONTALVO

Saratoga-Los Gatos Road, Saratoga. (408) 867-3421. Arboretum: daily, 8-5. Galleries: daily except Mon., 1-4, 25¢.

Nature trails traverse a redwood grove, hills and meadows, and flower-covered arbors in this county-run arboretum. The villa's grounds are also a bird sanctuary for up to forty-one species of birds. The villa takes its name from a sixteenth-century Spanish author. Montalvo wrote a novel describing a tribe of Amazons living in a fabulous island paradise named "California!" The Amazons rode on gryphons, and the many stone gryphons on the grounds are sure to entrance youngsters.

PAUL MASSON VINEYARDS

13150 Saratoga Ave., Saratoga. (408) 257-7800. 10-4 daily. Free.

Display cabinets of rare wine vessels and glasses—some dating back to 1000 B.C.—and the slide show of the history of Paul Masson and his wine add information and pleasure to the self-guided tour offered here. In summers, there are jazz and classical music concerts on the grounds. There's a chess tournament in January and a champagne marathon run in July.

BILLY JONES WILDCAT RAILROAD

Oak Meadow Park, Los Gatos. (408) 349-9775. Daily except Mon., 11-5:30 in summer, and spring and fall weekends. Adults 50¢; under 16, 25¢.

A full steam narrow-gauge, eighteen-inch prairie-type railroad toots along a mile long track pulling four open cars. The short ride takes you into the forest, near a stream, and back to the busy city park.

LOS GATOS MUSEUM

Tait and Main Sts., Los Gatos. (408) 354-2646. 1-4 daily; Sun. 2-4. Tours by appointment. Free.

The art section of this welcoming museum features constantly changing historical and contemporary art exhibits. The natural history room has a fluorescent minerals exhibit and a table where you can touch petrified wood, talc, Indian mortars, and a fossil whale vertebra. The star of the show is the beehive. A glass cage surrounds this thriving hive on all sides except for the outer wall. You can stand for hours watching the bees fly in and out, filling and eating their honey comb. If you're very quiet, you can even hear them singing.

MISSION SANTA CLARA DE ASIS

University of Santa Clara, the Alameda, 820 Alviso, Santa Clara. (408) 984-4242. Daily, 7 a.m.-7 p.m. Free.

Founded in 1777 and now part of the university campus, the present mission is a replica of the third building raised on this site by the Mission fathers. An adobe wall from the original cloister still stands in the peaceful garden. The original cross of the Mission stands in front of the church, and the bell given by the King of Spain in 1778 still tolls.

The de Saisset Gallery (Tues.—Fri. 10-5; weekends 1-5) and *Ricard Observatory* (10-2 Wed.) are on the campus and make interesting short stops.

ROSICRUCIAN EGYPTIAN MUSEUM, SCIENCE MUSEUM & PLANETARIUM

Rosicrucian Park, Naglee and Park Avenues, San Jose. (408) 287-9171. Egyptian Museum: Tues.-Fri., 9-4:45; Sat.-Mon., 12-4:45. Free. Science Museum: Wed.-Sun., 1-5 in summer; weekends only in winter. Free. Planetarium shows: Mon.-Sat., 2 and 3:30, Sun., 1, 2:30 and 4. Planetarium itself is open on summer weekends, 12-5. Free. Adults, $1; ages 6-16, 50¢.

The wonderful, faraway world of ancient Egypt awaits to mystify and enchant you in a collection at least ten times larger than the King Tut show. Egyptian and Babylonian mummies, sculpture, paintings, jewelry, cosmetics, scarabs, scrolls, and amulets are here in abundance. The ornate coffins, mummified cats and falcons, and descriptions of the embalming process are totally absorbing. Our four-year-old kept wanting to know how "old" everybody was. A short tour takes you inside a rock tomb, the only one on the West Coast, through the outer hallways and into the crypt to see wall paintings, false doorways and the sarcophagus itself. Dioramas and lifelike models show the manner in which the ancient Egyptians lived.

There's a seismograph and a Foucault pendulum in the science museum next door, along with lifelike models of satellites, neighboring planets, moons and the solar system, with lots of buttons to push on exhibits demonstrating the fundamental laws of the physical sciences. Planetarium shows change regularly.

WINCHESTER MYSTERY HOUSE

525 South Winchester Blvd., San Jose. (408) 247-2000. Tours daily, 9-4:30 in winter, till 6 in summer. House and grounds: adults, $4.25; ages 5-12 $2.75. House tour: adults, $3.50; children $2. Both tours include the museum. Museum only: adults, $1; children 75¢.

Sarah Winchester, widow of the Winchester Rifle heir, was told that as long as she kept building something, she'd never die. So for thirty-eight years, carpenters worked twenty-four hours a day to build this one hundred-sixty room mansion, filled with mysteries. Doorways open to blank walls, secret passageways twist around, and the number thirteen appears everywhere — thirteen-stepped stairways, ceilings with thirteen panels, rooms with thirteen windows — all in the finest woods and crystals money could buy. The museum features life-size wax dioramas of the Winchesters and some of the people who used their hardware: Annie Oakley and Buffalo Bill, Butch Cassidy and the Sundance Kid, and Teddy Roosevelt.

HISTORIC SAN JOSE

635 Phelan Ave., Kelley Park, San Jose, (408) 287-2290. 10-4:30, Mon.–Fri.; 12-4:30 weekends. Adults, 25¢; children, 10¢; family, 50¢; under 8 and seniors free. Tours by appointment.

Historic San Jose offers a unique view of the past, a visit to the heart of San Jose much as it existed in the nineteenth century. On sixteen acres surrounding a quiet plaza, original and faithfully replicated homes and businesses present the past in a lively manner. O'Brien's Candy Store still serves candy and sodas; the print shop looks as if it could put out a paper tomorrow; the blacksmith works away in Dashaway Stables; and you can walk through or past the Bank of Italy, the Umbarger House, the 115-foot Electric Light Tower, the Firehouse, and the Doctor's office. The Pacific Hotel houses a "proper" museum tracing the people of the Santa Clara Valley, from the Ohlone Indians, to the Spanish and Mexican *vaqueros* and *rancheros*, and the Yankee pioneers. Chinatown San Jose, an 1885 nickelodeon and a nickel movie of the San Francisco earthquake are shown, along with a slanted narrow ladder once used in the New Almaden quicksilver mine.

(True history buffs will want to drive over to see the *Roberto Adobe*, built in 1836, at 770 Lincoln Avenue, and the *Peralta Adobe*, at 184 W. St. John Street, built in 1775, the sole structure remaining from the Spanish period.)

Greeting a Guardian at the Rosicrusian Museum.

JAPANESE FRIENDSHIP TEA GARDEN

1490 Senter Road, Kelley Park, San Jose (408) 294-4706. Tues.–Fri. 10-6, weekends until 5:30 or later, in summer. Free.

This tranquil garden is patterned after the Korakuen garden in San Jose's sister city of Okayama. The three lakes are designed to symbolize the word "kokoro," which means "heart-mind-and-soul." Picturesque bridges and waterfalls, shaped rocks and trees, and land and waterflowers are wonderful to wander around. Naturally, the children will head over to watch the families of *koi*, magnificent, fat gold, white and/or black carp who come when dinner is offered.

From the Tea Garden or the Historical Museum, you can take the *Southern Pacific Coast Rail Road Train* through Kelley Park to the next stop. Trains leave every half hour on the hour and the rides are 50¢.

HAPPY HOLLOW PARK & BABY ZOO

Kelley Park, Keyes and Senter Roads, San Jose. (408) 292-8188/295-8383. Daily, 10-4; Sun. 11-6. Adults $1.25; children 75¢.

A miniature Viking shop, gingerbread house, and King Arthur's castle are some of the attractions in this delightful children's park. There are places to climb, crooked miles to walk, animals to pet, a happy-go-round or Danny the Dragon to ride, and puppet shows to laugh at. The Zoo is inhabited by dwarf zebras, lemurs, Scottish Highland cows, Barbados sheep, pigmy horses and goats which are all there to be petted. Birds, monkeys and seals are viewable in the beautifully landscaped zoo itself. Picnic areas are available in Kelley Park.

71

YOUTH SCIENTIFIC INSTITUTE

Alum Rock Park, San Jose. (408) 258-4322. Tues.–Fri., 9-4:30; Sat., 12-4:30. Adults 25¢, children 10¢, families 50¢. (On summer Sundays, 12-4:30.)

A small petting area and a hands-on exhibit of whale bones and shark teeth will draw the children, as will the hawks, owls, ravens, kestrels, snakes, newts, skunks, boa constrictors, chinchillas, and chipmunks.

FRONTIER VILLAGE

4885 Monterey Rd. (Hwy. 82) San Jose. (408) 225-6015. Winter, weekends and holidays only, 10-5; summer: Mon.– Thurs., 10-5, Fri. and Sat., 10-10, Sun. 10-7. Admission packages from $5.25 to $6.95.

The family will have a great, fun-filled day at this Western amusement park. You can ride a stagecoach, an Old 99 train, or an Indian canoe, try your hand at trout fishing, visit Indian dwellings, and an 1890s school-house, and shoot around on the Apache whirlwind roller coaster. Noisy gunfights are staged in the middle of the street. There are regular Wild West shows and saloons that serve ice cream, sarsaparilla and Dixieland music. Picnic spots are available too. It's hard not to have a really good time here.

NEW ALMADEN MUSEUM

21570 Almaden Road, New Almaden. (408) 268-7869. Mon., Thur. and Fri. 1-4, Sat., Sun. and holidays, 10-5

Greeting the new arrivals in Frontier Village.

72

and by appointment. Adults, $2, Seniors, $1.75, children, 75¢.

The New Almaden mine was the first mercury mine in California. The woman who owns the mine has gathered together mementos of the Indians, Mexicans and American pioneers who lived in the area. She gives tour-talks through the museum, telling stories about the Indian dresses and artifacts, miners' tools and lunch pails, antique toys, sample ores, and old Mexican keepsakes. The barrel organ used by the padres to attract the Indians is of special interest.

FLYING LADY No. II AND WAGONS TO WINGS COLLECTION

Hill Country Showplace Golf Course, 15060 Foothill Road, Morgan Hill. (408) 779-4136. 12-3 and 5-9:30 Fri. and Sat.; 12-2:30 Wed. and Thur., 5-8 Wed., Thur. and Sun.; 12-3 Sat. and Sun.

The Flying Lady restaurant is remarkable for its relaxing golf-course setting and the model plane and picture collection covering its walls and ceiling. Two large buildings on the property house phenomenal collections of planes and wagons. We found a 1920 Briggs and Stratton Flier that got one hundred miles per gallon, a 1928 Gypsy Moth, a hupmobile, biplanes, war planes, jet planes, and a one-man folding helicopter. Buckboards, a graceful white hearse, a popcorn vender, stagecoaches, surreys, a dairy cart, and more are in the "horse-drawn" barn.

Further down 101, in Gilroy, you may want to stop in at the *Gilroy Historical Museum (195 Fifth St., (408) 847-2685, 10-4 except Tues. and Sun. Donation.)* to see its collection of local remembrances and Native American artifacts.

LICK OBSERVATORY

Mount Hamilton, Hwy. 130, 25 miles southeast of San Jose. (204) 274-5061 (recording), 429-2513. Visitors gallery 10-5 daily. Free. Tours, 1-5. Closed holidays.

A long narrow, winding road takes you to the top of Mount Hamilton and the awesome domes of Lick Observatory. It was here that the fifth moon of Jupiter was discovered—the first new one since the time of Galileo. The visitor's gallery looks up at one of the largest telescopes (120 inches) in the world, and the tour of photos and the telescopes, astronomical instruments and 36-inch refractor is intriguing and educational. Star gazing is possible for the public on Friday nights in summer, but you must write, enclosing a self-addressed, stamped envelope, for up to six tickets, in advance to Visitors Program, Lick Observatory, Mt. Hamilton, CA 95140.

PUBLIC RELATIONS TOURS

ACRES OF ORCHIDS. Rod McLellan Orchidary. 1450 El Camino Real, South San Francisco. (415) 871-5655. Guided tours 10:30 and 1:30 daily. Greenhouses open 8-5 daily. Orchids in more colors, types and sizes than you can imagine are here in varying stages for looking, smelling and buying.

PACIFIC PRESS PUBLISHING ASSOCIATION. 1350 Villa Street, Mountain View. (415) 961-2323. Free tours weekdays by appointment. Learn how books are made and see editors, artists and binders at work.

EDELWEISS DAIRY. 17717 Old Mountain View Road, Santa Clara. (408) 984-8484 Mon.–Sat., 9-5 by appt. Free. Here you'll see the milking process from cow to carton.

SAN MATEO TIMES. 1080 S. Amphlett Blvd., San Mateo. (415) 348-4321. Mon. and Wed.–Fri. 12-3:30 and by appointment. Free. Tour through every department to see the complete process of publication. Call one week in advance.

U.S. WEATHER SERVICE. Bayshore Freeway, San Bruno. San Francisco International Airport. (415) 876-2886. Free tours, by appointment.
   See the materials used in briefing pilots and the weather teletypes and instruments. To see San Francisco Airport itself, call 761-0800 for a ninety-minute tour.

PALO ALTO AIRPORT. 1901 Embarcadero Road, Palo Alto. (415) 856-7833. By appointment. Free.
   You can even get into the control tower if you make an additional call and appointment at 865-1277.

FRITO-LAY POTATO CHIPS. 650 N. King Road, San

A happy rider in Frontier Village.

Jose. (408) 251-8080. Wed. Write for reservations. Free.

Thirty-minute tours show how potato chips are made.

SUNSET MAGAZINE. Middlefield and Willow Roads, Menlo Park, (415) 321-3600. Tours Mon.–Fri. 10:30, 11:30, 1, 2 and 3. Gardens open 9-4:30. Free.

Cliff May designed the Sunset buildings to give the staff a good view and prevent glare. The garden itself is what the children like best: they can walk from one end to the other and view, in order, the botanical life of the western coast of America—the desert plants of Baja, the cactus of Southern California, the coastal shrubs of Monterey, the rhododendrons and sturdy trees of Oregon and Washington. Youngsters with an interest in journalism will learn that working on a magazine is not all glamour.

NASA AMES RESEARCH CENTER. Moffett Field, Mountain View. (415) 965-6497. By appt. Free.

A thirty-minute film and walking tour of the wind tunnel, space vehicles and other research facilities can be fascinating. At certain times, you can also see the centrifuge and flight operations.

6

THE SANTA CRUZ AREA

The Santa Cruz Area is small, nestled west of San Jose and north of Monterey. Big Basin Redwoods, Boulder Creek, and Loch Lomond are some of the natural sites of interest, and the villages of Watsonville and Castroville, home of the artichoke, are warm and welcoming. In Santa Cruz, beaches are the major interest. Be sure to have some car games with you—the drive from San Francisco can be long and slow.

SANTA CRUZ BEACH—BOARDWALK

Riverside Ave. and Beach Street, Santa Cruz. (408) 423-5590. Daily, 11-11 in summer, weekends 11-11 on Saturday, 11-7 on Sunday. Closed Christmas weekend.

Our eleven-year-old nephew calls the Giant Dipper roller coaster "a must." That's what I say about the 1911 merry-go-round with the authetic pipe organ and real brass rings. Last of the old-time boardwalks, Santa Cruz has everything you would hope to find on one: a Ferris wheel, bumper cars, skeet ball, miniature golf, a penny arcade, cotton candy, candied apples, corndogs, tacos, and gentle and stomach-churning rides. Crowds and prices change with the seasons.

The sand on the beach is white and welcoming and leads to the Santa Cruz Wharf, a great spot to fish and watch seals snoozing on the wharf pilings.

The pretty little lighthouse on Lighthouse Point marks the boundary of the Pacific Ocean and Monterey

Bay and shelters a tiny museum which is open weekend afternoons.

THE MYSTERY SPOT

1953 Banciforte Drive, Santa Cruz, (408) 423-8897, 9:30-4:30 daily. Adults $2, under 12, $1. Group rates.

All the laws of gravity seem to be challenged in this scary natural curiosity. Even the trees can't stand up straight, and a visitor always seems to be standing either backwards or sideways. One test here is to lay a carpenter's level across two cement blocks, checking to see that their tops are on the same level. Then stand on one and see your friend on the other suddenly shrink or grow tall. Our kids got a great kick out of walking up the walls of the cabin that looks cockeyed, but isn't.

SANTA CRUZ CITY MUSEUM

1305 East Cliff Drive, Santa Cruz. (408) 429-3773. Tues.–Sat., 10-5. Tourists, 50¢, residents 25¢, children and seniors free.

Baskets and artifacts from the Eskimo and California Indians and reminders of the Mission days are just part of this excellent collection. There are special changing exhibits, such as a microscope to use on feathers and shells, and a touchable exhibit of grinding rocks and acorn mash. There are mammoth tusks and a mastodon tooth. The Glenn W. Brandt Junior Museum Wing houses live and stuffed mammals, including a degus from Peru, the world's only small mammal with true color vision, birds, reptiles and insects. Turtle doves and golden eagles, geneological trees of the animal kingdom and a tidepool aquarium are children's favorites.

In town, the *Cooper House* in the Pacific Garden Mall is the old county courthouse transformed into a bazaar of shops that's a feast for the eye and the palate: cafes, a rainbow store, pet shop, and strolling musicians make it a good place to while away a rainy afternoon.

ROARING CAMP & BIG TREES NARROW GAUGE RAILROAD

Graham Hill and Mount Hermon Roads, Felton. (408) 335-4484. Winter: weekdays at noon, weekends and holidays at 12, 1:30 and 3. Spring and fall: weekdays at noon, weekends and holidays (and daily throughout the summer) at 11, 12:15, 1:30, 2:45 and 4 p.m. Closed Christmas Day. Moonlight parties, summer Saturdays and by appointment. Adults, $5.50; 3-15, $3.50.

Curving through redwood forests and over rattling wooden bridges, the original 1880 steam engine pulls old-fashioned excursion cars up and down hills and around sky-high trees. You can stop over at Bear Mountain to hike and picnic before returning to Roaring Camp on a later train. Back at the Camp, the shortest covered bridge in the world and a duck pond interest younger folk, while the Old General Store—offering pot-bellied stoves, cast-iron toys, stick candy and railroad books and magazines—intrigues the rest. Picnic tables and group rates are available.

THE VILLAGE

Hwy. 17, Scotts Valley. (408) 438-1000. Scheduled to open

in spring, 1981.

The Village is currently being transformed from Santa's Village to a larger, more general family amusement park. Rides, a puppet theater and a crafts square will be available.

TREE CIRCUS

4652 Scotts Valley Drive, Scotts Valley. (408) 438-3196. 10-5:30 daily. 75¢.

This mystery forest has appeared in "Believe It or Not" and *Popular Science* and is strangely interesting: seventy live trees have been carefully bent and twisted into geometric and pictorial shapes. The Double Spectacle Tree, Double-Heart Tree, Living Telephone Booth, and King's Throne are simply hard to believe.

CAPITOLA MUSEUM

410 Capitola Ave., Capitola (408) 476-5175. 9:30-4 weekdays. Free.

The Begonia Capital of the world (the Brown Bulb Ranch produces five million bulbs a year and with others in Capitola is responsible for 90 percent of the nation's supply of begonias) was once San Francisco's seaside resort because the railroad stopped here. This tiny museum celebrates that past with a wall covered by a painting of Capitola in 1884. Cameras, pictures, clothes and keepsakes are kept here as well.

WILLIAM H. VOLCK MEMORIAL MUSEUM

Pajaro Valley Historical Association. 261 E. Beach Street, Watsonville. (408) 722-0305. Sat. 1-4 and by appointment. Free.

This lovely old house is truly a community museum. One of the biggest treasures is a large 1887 photograph of two young girls—who are now members of the historical society. Reticules, bisque dolls, glove boxes used by the ladies of the town, and a photo of the first telephone office in Watsonville are part of the changing displays. Two old candy jars still filled with forty-year-old candy always capture the children's attention.

7

THE MONTEREY AREA

The Monterey area is many things—it's an Arcadian seashore, a farm-rich industrial city, and a sweeping, windswept valley. Monterey is also the site of the first important Spanish settlement in California, and it was here that the state of California became part of the United States. Big Sur has probably the most magnificent seacoast in the U.S. Salinas, the city most of us know from Steinbeck's *East of Eden*, has fascinating industrial tours and many memories of Steinbeck himself. And the valley that sweeps south to Soledad Mission, past Pinnacles National Monument and on past San Antonio de Padua Mission, is just now being developed as fertile farm land. A day, or a weekend, in this area could never do it justice.

SAN JUAN BAUTISTA STATE HISTORIC PARK

San Juan Bautista. (408) 623-4881. 10-4:30 daily in winter, until 5 in summer. Adult ticket, usable in all state parks that day, 50¢.

A mission, a museum, an adobe house, an 1870s hotel and stables, a wash house, blacksmith shop, granary and wine-tasting room all encircle the lovely plaza of San Juan Bautista, representing three periods in California history—Spanish, Mexican and early Californian.

Start your visit at the Mission, founded in 1797 and carefully preserved. The old adobe rooms house many treasures, including a 1737 barrel organ, gaming sticks of the San Juan Indians, the original kitchen, and rawhide thongs and hand-shaped nails from the original building, and the original bells still call parishoners to daily mass. The rose gardens and olive groves are peaceful retreats, as is the Indian burial ground behind the church. The church itself is bright and colorful, painted by a sailor who jumped ship and became the first American citizen to settle in California.

Across the plaza is the *Zanetta House*, which once housed the Indian maidens of the settlement. The second floor was used as a public meeting room and dance hall. Visitors see fine china on the dining room table, a unique rocker in the living room, and furnished bedrooms. Pass the wash house and adobe cottage to the *Livery Stables*, where you can have fun rummaging through an assortment of carriages, wagons, harnesses, and mail pouches. The stables also house General Castro's secretary's office. *The Plaza Hotel*, next, is noted for its barroom, with billiard tables and poker tables standing ready. Built in 1813 as a barracks for the Spanish soldiers, the walls now display Wells Fargo memorabilia and photos and drawings of Indians, outlaws, and Mexican and Yankee pioneers.

The *Castro House* should serve as a model for other museums: every room is completely labeled, with pictures to aid in the identification of its objects. The house is furnished as it was in the 1870s by the Breen family, who survived the Donner Party disaster to find a fortune in the gold fields. You'll see the candlesticks that came West with the Breens and diary, wardrobe, wedding dress, gloves, fan, orange blossoms, and card case of Isabella Breen. The kitchen is complete, down to the mouse trap on the floor and the laundry board in the sink.

The streets near the Plaza are full of old adobes and small interesting shops and restaurants, making San Juan Bautista a perfect place to spend a relaxing day.

SAN LUIS RESERVOIR

Romero Overlook. Hwy. 152, between Hollister and Los Banos. (209) 826-09718 x253. 9:30-5:30, weekends, 9-5 weekdays. Closed holidays.

The history of this $600-million project is spread out before you, from Indian artifacts found during the digging of the dam, to the plant and viewing window of the generator. Movies and slide shows on water conservation and the water project are shown, and a ranger will answer questions.

MONTEREY

Monterey's recorded history started when Cabrillo sighted the Bay of Piños in 1542. Today it's a bustling town ringing with history and always looking at the bay.

Fisherman's Wharf is a mélange of restaurants, fish stores, and shops. Fishing and seal watching are favorite pastimes and you can go for a boat ride or take a diving bell thirty feet down to look at the ocean's floor.

Cannery Row is a far cry from the Cannery Row John Steinbeck told us about. This is a growing complex of restaurants, shops and galleries offering entertainment for all. It's here you'll find "The Funniest Place in Town!"—the *Edgewater Packing Company* and its 1905 Colossal Carrousel (640 Wave Street, (408) 649-1899, 8 a.m.-11 p.m., longer hours on summer weekends.). You can ride a unicorn, listen to the loud calliope and look at the sea on the carrousel's surprisingly fast, long ride. On the other side of the arcade is a restaurant, ice cream and pie shop, with fifteen kinds of pie and cake and deliciously old-fashioned ice cream concoctions. The flaming banana split is $2.95 and is served in a ceramic banana. Kids' parties are held in the old fire engine.

SANCHO PANZA RESTAURANT

Casa Gutierrez, 590 Calle Principal. Monterey. (408) 375-0095. 11-2, 5-9. Open later on summer weekends.

Built in 1841 by a young Mexican for his bride, the old adobe is now a comfortable Mexican country inn that looks like an early Monterey home. A warm fire blazes on cool evenings and there's a garden in back for lunch and summer nights. Prices are reasonable and the food is very good. Cool wine is poured from huge kegs near the door. Mexican-American newspapers are used as placemats and conversation pieces. At the end of the meal, top it off with Chocolato Mejicano—crushed almonds and cinnamon in frothy hot chocolate.

ALLEN KNIGHT MARITIME MUSEUM

550 Calle Principal. Monterey. (408) 375-2553. Tues.- Fri. 1-4; Weekends, 2-4. Free.

A captain's cabin from an old sailing ship with bed, writing desk and sailor's ditty box, sets the proper mood for this nautical museum. Models, photos, lithographs, paintings and various old sailing materials, octants, ships' bells, sailors' thimbles, Arctic goggles, scrimshaw and ships' logs are some of the items on display. One exhibit pictures all the ships that have visited Monterey harbor. There's even a sardine boat in which you can pretend you're sailing.

THE LARKIN HOUSE

Jefferson Street and Calle Principal. Monterey. (408) 649-2837. 35-minute guided tours from 9 to 4. Garden open until 5. Adult state parks ticket, 50¢.

Built by Thomas Oliver Larkin, first and only U.S. Consul to Mexico stationed in Monterey, the house is an architectural and historical gem. It was the first home in Monterey to follow the New England style as well as the first to have glass windows. Many of the furnishings are original Larkin items.

Through the rose-covered garden is a small house used by William Tecumseh Sherman, an army lieutenant in 1847-9. The house now serves as a waiting room for the Larkin House tour and as a small museum of Sherman's and Larkin's roles in California history. Here you learn that Sherman promised to return to lovely Doña Maria Ignacio Bonifacio. She planted a rose to bloom when he returned. And although the Sherman rose has bloomed yearly ever since, the man who marched through Georgia never returned.

On the next block, the *Cooper-Molera House* (at the corner of Polk and Munras) will soon be open to the public. John B. R. Cooper, trader and sea captain, came to Monterey in the 1920s, married the daughter of Ignacio Vallejo, and founded a dynasty of farm, ranch and vineyards. His granddaughter bequeathed the property to the nation.

THE STEVENSON HOUSE

530 Houston Street, Monterey. (408) 649-2836. Tours every hour on the hour, 9-4. Adult state parks ticket, 50¢, usable at all state parks that day.

Robert Louis Stevenson spent a few months in a second-floor room of this boarding house during 1879. He had traveled from Scotland to visit Fanny Osbourne, who later became his wife. He wrote *The Old Pacific Capital* here and the house, restored to look as it did then, is filled with Stevenson memorabilia. Upstairs, at the foot of the bed in the children's room, a ghostly spirit is sometimes spotted. The lovely garden makes a nice waiting room for the tour.

COLTON HALL

Dutra and King Streets, Monterey. (408) 646-3750. 10-5, Tues.–Sun. Free.

Colton Hall, the first town hall and public school of Monterey is famed as the site, in 1849, of the first Constitutional Congress of the new State of California. Here, the California Constitution was written in Spanish and English and the Great Seal of the state was designed. The large meeting room is furnished as it was then, with biographies and portraits of each of the men who signed the constitution, including Larkin, Vallejo, Ellis, Sutter, and Ord. A twenty-six-star flag flies.

Behind Colton Hall is the old *Monterey Jail*, open daily until 4:30. The walls are thick stone, the doors iron and the cells pitch black and scary. It is impossible to believe that this was used as the city jail until May, 1959, but that's what the sign says.

THE CUSTOM HOUSE

1 Custom House Plaza. 115 Alvarado Street, Monterey. (408) 649-2836. 9-5 daily. Free.

The United States flag was first officially raised in California on this roof in 1846. Today, you walk into a long room that holds the exact duplicate of the cargo Richard Henry Dana wrote about in his *Two Years Before the Mast*. There are casks of liquor, cases of dishes, bags of nails, coffee, flour, and wagon wheels. A screeching yellow and green parrot lords over ribbons, ropes, cloth, soap, paper, tools, and trunks. In one corner are piles of "California bank notes"—the cowhides used for trading. The Custom House manager's quarters upstairs features a comfortable carved bed and chest, a table and a desk with an open book and a cigar ready to be lit.

PACIFIC HOUSE MUSEUM

8 Custom House Plaza, Monterey. (408) 649-2837. 10-5 daily. Adult state parks ticket, 50¢

The first floor of this tavern-court-newspaper-church-ballroom is now a museum of California history with artifact-filled cases arranged chronologically, beginning with the Costanoan Indians. Spanish saddles and money, gold miners' tools, a whaling boat, and the

Victorian furniture of the pioneers are all here.

Upstairs is the Holman Collection, a remarkable gathering of Indian relics from all over North America. Costanoan religion, hunting, fishing, gathering, and processing of acorns, housing, trade, warfare, transportation and survival lessons are explained with artifacts and models. Visitors can compare the arrows, games, beads, and baskets of many tribes, from Alaskan Eskimos to American Indians.

CASA DEL ORO

Scott and Olivier Streets, Monterey. (408) 649-2837. 9-5 daily. Free.

Thomas Larkin built this trading store in 1845. During the gold rush, when the big iron safe stored the miners' gold, the building became known as The House of Gold. Visitors can stand at the door to look at this fully equipped general store of the last century. Sewing machines and furniture are piled high, with chairs hanging from the rafters. Bags of coffee, bolts of cloth, cans of milk, and barrels of food all wait for customers. Located between the Pacific Building and the First Theater, Casa del Oro offers a few interesting minutes.

CALIFORNIA'S FIRST THEATER

Scott and Pacific Streets, Monterey. (408) 649-2837. 9-5 except Mon. and Tues. Adult ticket, 50¢ usable at all state buildings that day. Box office: Wed.–Sun. 1-8, 375-4916.

Jack Swan's lodging house gave its first performance of a stage play in 1847 to entertain bored soldiers. Since then, theatrical productions have been produced regularly and now nineteenth-century melodramas are performed on weekends. During the day, a ranger shows you through the theater and tells you about what you'd like to know. He'll tell you that they used to serve hot peanuts until the villain of the plays complained about being hit, that Lola Montez visited Monterey (and why), and where Swan got his 1800 hurdy-gurdy. Several present-day movie heroes made their acting debuts here with the Troupers of the Gold Coast. If you look carefully, you can spot them on recent billboards.

Two new buildings have just been made available to the public on the block next to the First Theater, *The Old Whaling Station* and the *First Brick House.* The Old Whaling Station, located between Pacific Street and Custom House Plaza, was modeled after the owner's 1840 Scots home. As headquarters for Portuguese whalers in the 1850s, the beach was soon known for the whale oil rendering. A whalebone walk in front of the house is a reminder of those days. The First Brick House was built by Gallant G. Dickenson, who fired his own bricks in 1846, prospered in the gold country, and served as a delegate to the California Constitutional Convention. Both buildings are part of California's State Parks Dept.

CASA SOBRANES

Pacific and Del Monte, Monterey. (408) 649-2837. Sat.– Wed., tours on the hour from 9 to 4. Adult state parks ticket 50¢.

"The House with the Blue Gate" is a unique example of intermingling of architecture of Southern Spain and New England during Monterey's prosperity under Mexican rule.

U.S. ARMY MUSEUM

The Presidio, Monterey. (408) 242-8414. Thurs.—Mon. 9-12:30 and 1:30-4. Free.

This Army-run museum displays the history of old Fort Hill from the Ohlone Indian period to the present. Monuments to Commander John Drake Sloat and Father Junipero Serra adjoin the museum. Ten history sites are located nearby: Rumsen village sites and ceremonial rock; Father Serra's landing place, and the ruins of the first American fort in Monterey. The museum collection includes uniforms from the turn of the century, saddles, swords, sabers and other army equipment and dioramas of early forts and the first Presidio.

PACIFIC GROVE MUSEUM OF NATURAL HISTORY

Forest and Central Avenues, Pacific Grove. (408) 372-4212. Daily except Mon., 10-5. Free.

Each October, thousands of Monarch butterflies arrive in Pacific Grove to winter in a grove of pine trees until March. Visitors who arrive in other months, and don't want to climb a pine tree, can see a marvelous exhibit of the Monarch in this museum. There is also a large collection of tropical and other California butterflies, as well as Monterey sea otters, fish, mammals, rodents, insects, and birds, stuffed and in photos. The skeleton of a sea otter playing with a clamshell is particularly touching.

POINT PIÑOS LIGHTHOUSE

Off 17 Mile Drive. Pacific Grove. (408) 373-3304. 1-4 weekends in summer. Free.

The oldest lighthouse (1855) on the West Coast, Point Piños overlooks the meadows and sand dunes of a golf course on one side and a white-capped ocean on the other. A small U.S. Coast Guard maritime museum is open to the public upstairs, and downstairs a modern computer-operated signal is sent out to fog-bound ships.

Nearby, on the way into town, Lovers Point offers marine gardens, a small rocky beach, tree-shaded picnic grounds, and glass-bottomed boats in summer.

MISSION SAN CARLOS BORROMEO

Rio Road off Hwy. 1, Carmel. (408) 624-3600. Weekdays 9:30-4:45; Sun. and holidays, 10:30-4:45. Donation.

This lovely mission church and cemetary, two museums, and the adobe home of the pioneer Munras family combine to make this mission a "must stop." Father Junipero Serra rests in the church and in the cemetery lies Old Gabriel, 151 years old, baptized by Father Serra. A small museum in the garden houses pictures of the original mission and its restoration. There are Indian grinding pots, arrowheads, baskets, beads, toys, and two Indian skeletons buried with eagle claws and turtles. The long main museum offers fine art from the original mission and a replica of the stark cell Father Serra died in. You'll also find California's first library here—Father Serra's books, Bibles, theologies, sermons, travel commentary, lives of the saints, and technical works. Altar pieces, saddles, the furnished kitchen and dining room, and some of the mission priests' vestments are here, too.

The *Casa Munras* is now a memorial to the Munras family. There are keys from the original adobe, embroidery, family pictures, music and provision boxes, jewelry, maps, chocolate pots, and dresses. The Munras living room is furnished with a cradle and doll buggy, Victorian ornaments, a marble fireplace and handsome carved furniture.

POINT LOBOS STATE RESERVE

Rt. 1, South of Carmel. (408) 624-4909. 9-4 daily in winter, later in summer. Cars, $1.50.

The harsh barking of the sea lions offshore gives the name to this rocky and sea-ravaged point of land—"Punta de los Lobos Marinos," or Point of the Sea Wolves. You can still hear the sea lions and see them frolicking on the rocks on lucky days. Point Lobos is an outdoor museum: each tree, plant and shrub is identified and protected by law, as are the cormorants, pelicans, squirrels, and black-tailed deer that live here. The last natural grove of Monterey cypress stands here. Picnics and water sports are allowed in marked areas and several trails have detailed brochures to accompany you on your self-guided tour.

CARMEL

A visit to the Monterey Peninsula is not complete without an hour or two of browsing in the picturesque village of Carmel. The Pine Inn Block, bounded by Ocean Avenue, Lincoln, Monte Verde and Sixth Avenue, is an ever-changing scene of Victorian shops, gardens and restaurants. Of special interest to the children: Sylvia's Danish Pastry Shop (Sixth and Dolores, (408) 624-1198) for creamy goodies; the Gallery of Fine Comic Art (Seventh and Mission, 624-3278); and Thinker Toys (Carmel Plaza, 9 to 9 daily, Sun. 10-5:30) for a den of games, educational and imported toys, puppets and dollhouse furnishings. The Mediterranean Market at Ocean and Mission supplies picnic items for your walk on Carmel Beach, at the end of Ocean Avenue, one of the most beautiful on the coast.

THUNDERBIRD BOOK SHOP AND RESTAURANT

The Barnyard, Carmel Valley. (408) 624-1803. 10-9:30 in summer, in winter 10-5:30 weekdays, Sunday 11-5.

The Thunderbird is just what you dream a bookstore might be—a place where browsing is welcomed and the selection of books for children and adults is phenomenal. One corner of the store is a restaurant, serving lunch every day and dinner Tuesday through Saturday. Chess and checker boards are on some tables.

THE STEINBECK HOUSE

132 Central Avenue, Salinas. (408) 757-3106. Tours by appointment.

John Steinbeck's childhood Victorian home is now a luncheon restaurant with seatings at 11:45 or 1:15, Monday through Friday. The refurbished home offers fresh produce of the valley amid Steinbeck memorabilia. Profits go toward the Valley Historical Guild restorations. Reservations are necessary.

The *Steinbeck Library*, at 110 W. San Luis, displays

an extensive collection of John Steinbeck's memorabilia, including reviews and personal correspondence, and a lifesize bronze statue.

BORONDA ADOBE

Boronda Road at W. Laurel Drive. Salinas. (408) 424-7155. Tue., Thur., and Sat., 1-4. Free.

The home of Don Manuel de Boronda, a native of Spain who came to California as a corporal in the early 1800s is now a museum of Monterey County. Lettuce brands, silent movies of early lettuce farming, Native American baskets, mortar and pestles of Stone Age Man, old election posters, railroad tools, and tokens of the lettuce farmers mix with letters, artifacts, and photos of the Boronda family. Picnic areas are available.

In town, the *First Mayor's Home*, at 238 E. Romie (422-1150, 1-4 weekends and by appointment) is a Victorian-restoration project now in progress.

ISSEI PIONEER MUSEUM

14 California Street, Salinas. (408) 424-4105. By appointment only.

The first Issei pioneer museum in the United States, housed in the annex of the Buddhist Temple, contains over six hundred items donated by Issei (first generation of Japanese to emigrate to the U.S.) and their descendants. Many of the articles were handmade by the Issei during W.W. II in Arizona and California relocation camps. The oldest item is a book about Tokyo, printed in 1850.

MISSION NUESTRA SEÑORA DE SOLEDAD

Soledad, Hwy. 101. (408) 678-2586. 10-4 except Tues. Free.

Founded in 1791, Soledad is the last mission to have been restored. It's now a lovely oasis in a windswept valley. Visitors can visit the museum and chapel and then spend time in the gift shop, graveyard and picnic area.

PINNACLES NATIONAL MONUMENT

Off 101 at King City. (408) 389-4578. $1.50 per car per day.

Entered from Soledad or King City, Pinnacles National Monument is a little-known land of striking beauty. Its 14,000 acres are comparable in rock formations and color striations only to the Grand Canyon. The fern glens, caves, wild animals, and the curious pinnacles themselves, some rising 1,200 feet above the canyon floors, make this a perfect hiking spot in spring and fall.

SAN ANTONIO DE PADUA MISSION

Jolon. (Off Hwy. 101 from King City) 9-4:30 daily. Donation. (408) 385-4478.

In its Valley of the Oaks, San Antonio de Padua is one of the most interesting of the California missions. It still functions as a working mission, with olive and vine presses, fields planted and stock roaming the hills, just as it did in 1771, but on a much smaller scale. Inside the mission museum, you can walk through the candle- and soap-making rooms, visit a sample mission bedroom and the kitchens and climb up to the original wine vat. Unfortunately, vandals have destroyed the beehive ovens, Temescal sweat houses and aqueduct system once on the grounds. Steinbeck described the mission—abandoned during a drought—in *To a God Unknown*.

PUBLIC RELATIONS TOURS

PETER PAUL CANDY FACTORY. 1800 So. Abott, Salinas. (408) 424-0481. Tues. and Thur. at 10 a.m. and by appointment. Free. For children over eight.

It's hard to believe this beautifully designed building is a factory, but it's a candy manufactory, with the most tantalizing smells. Before the tour white bakers' hats are passed out as souvenirs. The tour winds around vats of chocolate, sugar and corn syrup, under conveyor belts of coconut and rice crispies, past mixers and steam-jacketed kettles and into a room where almonds are shaken, dusted, roasted and chocolate-covered. Every day the Peter Paul factory uses 26,000 pounds of chocolate. At the end of the tour, candy bars satisfy your craving.

SCHILLING SPICES—McCORMICK AND CO. 1311 Schilling Place, Salinas. (408) 758-2411. Tues. and Thurs. at 1 p.m. and by appointment. (Children of junior high age and older only.)

Visitors see spices cleaned, processed, mixed, packaged, labeled, and boxed. Small samples (we got a mixture for salads) are presented at the end of the tour.

HOERNER-WALDORF CORP. 1078 Merrill, Salinas. (408) 424-1831. Nov.-April, by appointment for children over 10.

Visitors see manufacturing of corrugated boxes and paper laminations.

SALINAS VALLEY WAX PAPER COMPANY. 1111 Abbott Street, Salinas. (408) 424-2747. By appointment.

Huge rolls of paper are cut and shredded, foil is laminated and paper is waxed here.

ROD McLELLAN CO. 2352 San Juan Rd., Watsonville, CA 95076. Sat. and Sun. 10:30 and 1:30 and by appointment.

Acres of roses, orchids and gardenias fill the one hundred greenhouses you can tour through here.

MONTEREY PENINSULA HERALD NEWSPAPER. Pacific and Jefferson Streets, Monterey. (408) 372-3311. Tours by appointment.

SALINAS CALIFORNIAN NEWSPAPER. 123 W. Alisal, Salinas. (408) 424-2221 x70. Tours by appointment.

Visitors will see "Big Red," print 56,000 newspapers per hour, and editors, writers and typesetters gathering news, producing, and printing the newspaper.

8

THE EAST BAY—ALAMEDA AND CONTRA COSTA COUNTIES

The East Bay, ranging along the east shore of San Francisco Bay, is a green land dotted with public parks and streams and crowned by Mt. Diablo. The places of interest in this area are some distance from each other, so it's advisable to plan ahead. The Berkeley hills across the bay from San Francisco and the Carquinez Straits frame the East Bay beautifully. Boaters, fishermen, picnickers, hikers and nature lovers of all ages will find special places to visit here.

NAVY MARINE CORPS MUSEUM

Building 1, Treasure Island. (415) 765-9111/832-7384. Daily, 10-3:30. Free.
 An immense, 251-foot long bicentennial mural by artist Lowell Nesbitt portrays the history of Navy and Marine activities in the Pacific, in eleven historic events. Displays from the Mexican War of 1840 and the Boxer Rebellion of 1853 are of interest, along with collections of Navy and Marine historical artifacts, model ships, 1939 Treasure Island Exposition tokens, and old uniforms.

JACK LONDON SQUARE

Foot of Broadway, Oakland.
 Busy waterfront stores and restaurants and a constantly changing view of ships in the Oakland estuary

make Jack London Square an interesting place for children to stroll around. At one end of the square is a special treasure—the Jack London Klondike Cabin, a small sod-covered cabin that housed Jack London in Yukon Territory during the Gold Rush in 1897. You'll see the crude furniture, rusty stove, shovels, snowshoes, gas lamps, pots and traps that Jack London used. The First and Last Chance saloon—in which Jack London is said to have imbibed—is nearby.

The *Bret Harte Boardwalk* a few blocks away is a pretty row of shops restored to their 1880s splendor.

THE GINGERBREAD HOUSE

741 Fifth Street (between Brush & Castro), Oakland. (415) 444-7373. Tues.–Thur., 11-6; Fri. and Sat. 11-7:30.

Hansel and Gretel's wicked witch would be envious of this tasty-looking shop and restaurant. Inside you'll find gingerbread cookies, puppets, dolls, aprons, potholders, cards, T-shirts—even gingerbread bubble bath. There's also a Black history collection and T. J. Robinson's old doll collection. Jambalaya, creole and cornbread are some of the Southern favorites served in the restaurant.

EAST BAY NEGRO HISTORICAL SOCIETY.

4519 Grove. Oakland. (415) 658-3158. Mon., Wed. and Fri., 12-5 and by appointment. Free.

California's Black Americans and their history is the theme of this lovingly put-together, information-crammed collection. The collection focuses on individual families, such as the William Sugg Family of Sonora—the donor's grandfather's freedom papers are framed on the wall; his grandmother was born in a covered wagon on the way to Gold Country in 1851 (their gold mining pan and a doll buggy from their house are there, too)—but black American athletes, musicians, scientists, and politicians are remembered, too. The three black miners who struck it rich and gave money for the Mt. Olivet Baptist Church in Marysville are remembered. So are the cowboys and farmers and doctors who are the forebears of Ruth Lasartemay who runs the museum. William Leidesdorff, treasurer of the town of San Francisco, James Beckworth, noted scout and explorer, Pio Pico, area founding father, and Colonel Allensworth, who founded a town near Fresno are all noted. Our favorite item is the christening dress of the child born to a lady-in-waiting to Queen Victoria who'd run off to the West Indies with the black coachman and then settled in San Francisco.

DUNSMUIR HOUSE & GARDEN

2960 Peralta Oaks Court (106 Avenue exit on Hwy. 580) May-Oct. Sundays, 12-4. Opens its Christmas display Thanksgiving week. House tour, $1; Garden tour, 50¢. (415) 562-9950.

If you'd like to see the movie set for "Burnt Offerings," and perhaps future Gothics, this is the place—it's just missing a few cobwebs. The stained glass domed roof and the music room are remarkable.

The nearby *Moss Cottage* (Mosswood Park), built in the mid-1800s, is a rare example of Gothic Revival Victorian, with arches, gables, spires, stained glass, and gingerbread echoing memories of days gone by.

THE OAKLAND MUSEUM

1000 Oak St., Oakland. (415) 273-3401. Tues.—Sat., 10-5; Sun. 12-7. Free.

Looking into the past in the Oakland Museum.

The Oakland Museum is three first-rate museums in one: California art, California history, and California natural sciences. You can always be sure of finding an afternoon's worth of interesting things for children of all ages.

The top level concentrates on California art from the days of the Spanish explorers to the present. Panoramic views of San Francisco, cowboys and Indians, Oriental art found in California homes, and modern canvases are all intriguing.

The natural sciences level includes exhibits on botany, birds, ecology, paleontology, and geology. An aquarium with everything from turkey fish to seahorses, and dioramas of mammals, birds, rodents, and snakes in their natural settings provide fascinating models of the real thing.

The California history level is perhaps the best of all. One begins with the Indians here in 3,000 B.C. and walks through "rooms" of the state's history, from the Spanish explorers, the Californios, to the gold miners and wild west cowboys, to the pioneers and turn-of-the-century Californians. The pioneer kitchen, with one chair of those grouped around the table actually outside the glass, so the young visitor can pretend he's in the kitchen, is one thing we always head for.

Concerts, films, and special exhibits on man and nature are scheduled regularly and the snack bar is open until 3:30.

93

CAMRON-STANFORD HOUSE

1418 Lakeside Drive, Oakland. (415) 836-1976. Wed. 11-4; Sun. 1-5. Free.

This 1876 Italianate-style Victorian provides a look at Oakland history since the days of the horse cars and gas lighting, when Lake Merritt was not a lake. Four rooms are furnished to reflect the local style of the Victorian era. Multi-media shows and special exhibits, and curators who point out the wooden columns made to look like stone and the furbelows and curleques produced by machine add to the young visitor's enjoyment.

LAKESIDE PARK

Off Grand Ave., Lake Merritt. Oakland. (415) 273-3091. 9-5 daily.

A narrow strip of grass around Lake Merritt offers peace in the center of a busy city. In the *Kiwanis Kiddie Korner*, children can slide down an octopus or swing on a sea horse.

The *Rotary Natural Science Center* (10-5 daily, 273-3739) shows free nature films on occasion, in addition to its regular fare of science exhibits and an aviary and zoo holding turkey vultures, barn owls, great horned owls, hawks, and sand-hill cranes, as well as possums, porcupines and skunks. This is the oldest wild life refuge in the U.S. and for 15¢ you can buy duck food to feed the free-flying waterfowl, which includes an occasional pelican.

Sailboats, houseboats, and paddleboats are offered for rent. *The Merritt Queen*, a replica of a Mississippi river boat takes half-hour tours of the lake (50¢ for adults, 35¢ for children and seniors) during summer vacations and on weekends.

The *Lakeside Toy Train* runs from 12:30-5:30 on weekends, depending on business. The round trip to Fairyland is 25¢ and takes fifteen minutes.

CHILDREN'S FAIRYLAND

Lakeside Park, Oakland. (415) 452-2259. Daily, 10-5:30, summer; Wed.—Sun., 10-5:30, spring and fall; weekends and holidays 10-4:40, winter. 50¢.

Duck through Mother Goose's Shoe to meet Alice, the Cheshire Cat, the Cowardly Lion, and the Queen of Fairyland. Then slide down a dragon's back, listen to the Bong Tree that chimes when you step on the secret spots, or sail on a pea green boat with the Owl and the Pussycat. Pinocchio, Willie the Whale, slides, mazes, rides and enchanted bowers come to life. All of the characters in Fairyland are here to make children smile and a magic key unlocks their stories (50¢). The seal food, Wonder-Go-Round and Magic Web Ferris wheel are nominally priced; puppet shows and clown shows are free.

OAKLAND ZOO AND BABY ZOO

Knowland State Park, MacArthur Freeway at Golf Links Road and 98th Avenue, Oakland. (415) 569-7353. 10-4:30 daily, longer hours on summer weekends. $1.50 per car. Baby Zoo: 569-8819, 10-4:30 daily. Adults, $1, under 14 and over 65, 50¢. Rides 25¢; train 35¢.

This beautifully arranged and landscaped zoo is one of the nicest in the state. The Jungle Lift can take you up over the African veldt, past the high ground where buffalo, deer and elk graze in a natural setting. A towering gibbon cage has a spiral walkway on which you can ascend all the way to the top to peek into the gibbon house. An elephant performs regularly.

In the Baby Zoo, children can feed and pet everything from baby lions, llamas and hippos, to pelicans, calves, seals, rabbits, swans, geese, and ponies. There are chickens and baby chicks, even the baby chimps romp with their own play chairs. Kids can take turns riding the giant Galapagos turtle. Watch out for the goats—they eat anything, even your name tags and your candy wrappers. (They might even nibble on your sleeve.)

MEEK ESTATE

Hampton and Boston Roads, Hayward. (415) 276-9844. House tours by appointment, 50¢; Garden park open daily, 9-dusk. Free.

Lovers of Victorian and nostalgia will love this totally furnished five-story 1869 national historic landmark. Visitors can "pretend" in the ballroom, library, solarium, bedrooms, a nursery, and servants' quarters. There are acres of park and playground equipment for pent-up energies, and a barbecue pit in the picnic area.

McCONAGHY ESTATE

18701 Hesperian Boulevard, Hayward. (415) 581-0223/ 278-0198. Thurs.—Sun., 1-4 and by appointment. Adults, $1, children, 50¢ (classes free). Special Christmas program in December.

An elegant 1886 farmhouse, furnished in keeping with the style in which it was built, a tank house, and a wagon and buggy-filled carriage house are handily located right next to Kennedy Park, with its picnic tables, merry-go-round and train.

CHABOT OBSERVATORY & PLANETARIUM

4917 Mountain Blvd. (near MacArthur Fwy. and Warren Blvd.), Oakland. (415) 531-4560. Fri. and Sat., 7:30 p.m. Children's program Sat. at 1. Adults, 50¢; children, 25¢. Reservations advised.

The changing two-hour show here includes a movie, science demonstration, and the planetarium program. A recent show presented an exciting space voyage and observation through a large telescope at the different solar systems. Youngsters learn how astronomers explore the universe and get a chance to observe the planets and stars through a telescope. Locating the Big and Little Dippers during the outdoor star gazing session is always a popular part of the show.

SULPHUR CREEK PARK

1801 D Street, Hayward. (415) 881-6747. Mon.—Sat., 10-5; Sun. 12-5. Free.

Sulphur Creek Park is a charming, out-of-the-way spot in which to introduce children to nature. Ducks roam freely near the creek and rustic, outdoor cages hold hawks, foxes, raccoons, ringtailed cats, coatis and opossum. Plants, trees and fungus-bearing logs are neatly labelled throughout the grounds. The small museum offers a question-and-answer exhibit on how snakes smell and birds eat, along with touchable items and a display of the oddities of nature. Local children can take advantage of the animal lending library to take home hampsters, rats, mice, rabbits, and guinea pigs.

HAYWARD AREA HISTORICAL SOCIETY MUSEUM

22701 Main, at C, Hayward. (415) 581-0223. 12-4, Mon.–Fri. and first Saturday of each month, 10-4. Free.

The large brick 1927 post office is now a lovingly presented album of Hayward history. Ladies' derringers and antique guns, cameras, dolls, baby buggies, teddybears, scrapbooks full of high school pictures, tax records and family albums, one thousand handkerchiefs, a steriopticon, a 1923 fire engine, an 1820s hand-drawn fire pumper that was shipped around the Horn to San Francisco in 1849, doctors and midwives' instruments, and post office, fire, police and veterans displays are a little overwhelming. The gracious curator enjoys playing the old phonographs for youngsters and telling them the stories behind these artifacts.

MISSION SAN JOSE

4330 Mission Blvd., Fremont. (415) 656-9125. 10-4:30 daily, in winter; until 5 in summer. Donation.

Founded in 1797, Mission San Jose has had an exciting place in California history. During the Gold Rush, it served as a trading post for miners, after surviving many years of Indian attacks. Father Duran, who arrived in 1806, taught some of the two thousand Ohlone neophytes to play the original Mission bells and

musical instruments now on display. Vestments worn by Father Serra, timbers and rawhides from the original mission building, an 1890s buggy, the original baptismal font, a pioneer cradle and the sanctus bells are housed in the adobe living quarters of the mission padres. The story of General Vallejo's older brother's life and the local Vallejo adobe is especially touching.

REFUGE HEADQUARTERS INTERPRETIVE CENTER

Hwy. 84 (Near Dumbarton Bridge toll plaza), Fremont. (415) 792-3178. Wed.–Sun., 10-5. Free.

Photographic exhibits on special environmental programs, nature study walks, slide and film programs and self-guided walks through the salt marsh and diked ponds at Newark Slough help introduce youngsters to the world around them.

ALAMEDA-LIVERMORE VALLEY MUSEUM

Alameda County Fairgrounds (Hwys. 580 and 680), Pleasanton. (415) 462-2766. Tues.–Fri., 1-4 and by appointment. Free.

A turn-of-the-century dentist's office, a cooperage, a blacksmith shop, and a 1930s kitchen attract youngsters in this pleasant museum. Changing exhibits—such as the one we saw on the Ohlone Indians—also keep their interest.

History buffs may want to visit the *Dublin Heritage Center* in the Old Murray School (6600 Donlon Way, 828-3377) now in the process of being restored.

LIVERMORE HISTORIC CENTER

2155 Third St., Livermore. (415) 449-9927. 11:30-4, Wed.–Sun. Free.

This teaching exhibit of the history of the Livermore Valley from prehistoric times to the present is housed in the old Carnegie Library. Fossilized oysters, pictures, maps, and artifacts from the local coal mines and fuse factory are on display, along with a uniform used in the recent re-enactment of the de Anza expedition. The museum members are currently working on the restoration of the Historical Hayward Garage, in Livermore, on North L and Portola, which will be a museum of local transportation.

Ravenswood, the Victorian cottage and gardens built by San Francisco's "Blind Boss" Buckley, is occasionally open to the public. (It's on Arroyo Road, call 447-7300 for an appointment.) Visitors may see cloisonné chandeliers, an ornate billiard table, clothing, pictures, and mementos of the Buckley family.

EAST BAY MODEL TRAIN ENGINEERS SOCIETY

4075 Halleck Street, Emeryville. (415) 658-3537. Open third Friday of the month and infrequently on weekends, 7:30-10 p.m. Adults, $1.50; children 50¢.

When you go through the caboose entrance you'll see the largest scale model railroad in the world—freight trains, steamliners, and more, set up in their own universe—well worth staying up one evening for.

Castro Point Railway Museum (Pt. Molate Park, Pt. Molate Road and Richmond Belt Railroad, near the toll gate of the San Rafael Bridge, Richmond. (415) 234-6473, first Sunday of the month, 10-4, and July 4. Donations.) runs trains with "O" steam locomotives, for one-half-hour trips.

UNIVERSITY ART MUSEUM

2626 Bancroft Way, Berkeley. (415) 642-1207. Wed.–Sun., 11-5. Free.

Berkeley's museum is a natural for children, not so much for the art but for the building itself. Its unique multileveled, concrete-slab construction enables a young visitor to see its spacious interiors from any of the many corners and balconies. The outdoor sculpture garden is fun and the primitive art usually strikes a chord with young people.

The Pacific Film Archive, located in the museum basement (642-1412/1124) shows old and rare films every evening.

McCALLUM'S FAMOUS ICE CREAM

1825 Solano, Berkeley. (415) 525-3510. Daily, 7 a.m.-11 p.m.; Fri. and Sat. till midnight.

McCallum's specializes in delicious and mountainous ice cream creations. Try the hot fudge sundae, served with a pitcher of hot sauce on the side, or the toasted almond chocolate shake in a tall glass lined with fudge. The Large McCallum's Nightmare serves four to eight for $18. The Sink, at $20, serves more—it has dozens of shovels of ice cream in many flavors and almost as many toppings. Everything is dished out by Scotch-garbed lads and lassies, and there are cones on the other side of the store for on-the-run tasting.

LAWRENCE HALL OF SCIENCE

Canyon Road, North and Grizzly Peak Boulevard, Berkeley. (415) 642-5132; Mon.–Fri., 10-4:30. Thurs. evening until 9. Sat. and Sun., 10-5. Adults $1.75. Students and seniors, 75¢.

Our ten- and twelve-year-old nephews had to be dragged away from this place at closing time. There are almost too many exhibits—science workshops, tests of your mathematical and logical ability, tests of knowledge, computers to play with, visual oddities that help you learn more about how your eyes work, and a hundred different mechanical things to tantalize and amuse. The Biology Lab is the place to investigate the world of living things (open weekends, 1-5). There is also an extensive mineral and gem collection and a grand view of the bay, the bridges and San Francisco.

LOWIE MUSEUM

Kroeber Hall, University of California, Berkeley. (415) 642-3681, Mon.–Fri., 10-4; weekends, 12-4. Adults,

50¢; children 25¢.

Across the street from the University Art Museum, a totem pole chronicles the family history of an Indian chief from the Queen Charlotte Islands and points the way to more archeological treasures. Permanent exhibits include photos of Ishi, things that Ishi made, and plaster casts of Pleistocene Man. "Life After Life" in Egypt is part of the rotating lifestyles and cultural exhibits.

THE CAMPANILE

Sather Tower, University of California, Berkeley. (415) 642-6000. Daily, 10-5, 10¢.

From the top of this tower, you can see San Francisco, Alcatraz, Mt. Tamalpais, the Golden Gate, and Bay Bridges and the entire campus. Above you twelve bronze bells weighing almost nine tons ring out melodies three times a day and you see them being played.

INTEGRAL URBAN HOUSE OF THE FARALLONES INSTITUTE

1516 Fifth Street, Berkeley, (415) 525-1150. Self-guided tours 10-3, Tues.–Fri. and Sat., 1-5, $1. Guided tours Sat., 1:15 and 2:30, and by appointment, $2.

The Integral Urban House is devoted to the study and demonstration of environmentally sound strategies and techniques of food production, energy conservation and generation, waste recycling, and pest management suitable for urban areas. From the alfalfa that's replaced the lawn to the solar hot water system and greenhouse, to the waterless toilet to the chicken coops, beehives and

fishponds, this city house may be the house of the future.

DIABLO VALLEY COLLEGE MUSEUM AND PLANETARIUM

321 Golf Club Rd., Pleasant Hill. (415) 684-1230. Museum: Mon., Wed. and Fri. 9:30-12, 1-4:30, Sat., 1:30-5. Planetarium shows Saturday at 3. Groups by appointment. Free.

In this museum youngsters can see a seismograph working, a Foucault pendulum swinging, and changing oceanography and anthropological exhibits on Native Americans. Local animals, especially the nocturnal moles, weasels and owls, are fun to see too.

TILDEN REGIONAL PARK & ENVIRONMENTAL EDUCATION CENTER

Canyon Drive off Grizzly Peak Boulevard, Berkeley. (415) 525-2233. Daily, except Mon., 10-5. Little Farm, daily, 8-5. Free. Rides are nominally priced.

Tilden Park has a pony ride, a historic merry-go-round, a duck pond, and a miniature train. Botanical gardens, a nature center, and swimming in Lake Anza are some of the other recreational facilities in this well-equipped park. But the chief attraction, especially for young people, is the Little Farm. Mary Ann the Mexican burro, Snuffy the sheep, Rosebud the pig, and Buttercup the cow are among the family members of this charming little farm. There are chickens, ducks and rabbits to feed and pet as well. Children are taught to walk toward the animals for petting and how to feed them (with a flat-tened hand and only the foods that are good for them).

ALEXANDER LINDSAY JUNIOR MUSEUM

1901 First Avenue, Walnut Creek. (415) 935-1978. Wed.–Fri., 1-5; Sat., 11-3. Free.

A miniature zoo housing touchable animals and birds, an aquarium of native fish and amphibians and a collection of rocks, fossils, shells and Indian artifacts are the main features of this small museum, which special-izes in caring for, and rehabilitating wounded birds of prey and wild animals. Coyotes, badgers, foxes, owls, hawks, skunks, vultures, badgers, boas and king snakes are a few of the animals on display. Some of the smaller domestic animals can be rented to be kept as pets for one dollar a year.

BLACK DIAMOND MINE REGIONAL PRESERVE

Follow Hwy. 4 to Somersville Road, head south to road's end. Antioch. (415) 757-2620. Weekends: 9:30-12 and 1:30-3. By reservation. Adults $1; children 50¢.

One-and-a-half- and two-and-a-half-hour tours take you down into a coal mine to see veins of coal and to learn about mining and area history. Then you hike up to a legend-filled graveyard.

JOHN MUIR NATIONAL HISTORIC SITE

4202 Alhambra Avenue, Martinez. (415) 228-8860. Tours

On horseback in Tilden Park.

The family rides Cinderella's coach in Happy Hollow.

daily on the hour, 8:30-4:30, except holidays. Ages 16-62, 50¢.

After a beautiful half-hour film narrated by John Muir's text and scenes of the natural wonders that inspired it, visitors go through Muir's large nineteenth-century farmhouse, which is one of the most authentically presented houses you can visit. Details such as closets filled with clothing, Muir's suitcase on the bed ready for travel and the glasses and pencils, books and papers standing ready on Muir's desk in his "scribble den," give the house a lived-in look. You can go up to the treasure-filled attic, from which Muir used to shout orders to his farmhands.

Also on the Muir property is the *Martinez Adobe*, which was built by the son of the Mexican don who built the town of Martinez. The thick-walled adobe has served as headquarters for the Rancho foreman's quarters on the Muir Ranch, and as the home of Muir's daughter and family. You may wander through the grounds to look at the exotic plants Muir gathered and stay as long as you like.

101

BENICIA CAPITOL STATE HISTORIC PARK

First and G Streets, Benicia. (707) 745-3385. 10-5 daily. Adult ticket, 50¢, usable at all state parks that day.

Benicia was the capitol of California for over a year, and the capitol building looks now as it did in 1854. The exhibit room provides the history of early California. Our fourth graders were fascinated with the whale oil lamps, quill pens and shiny brass cuspidors.

Across the colorful garden is the *Fischer-Hanlon House* (weekends, 12-4 and by appointment. 745-1554), a proper, middle-class merchant's home of the 1880s.

MURIEL'S DOLL HOUSE MUSEUM

33 Canyon Lake Drive, Port Costa. (415) 787-2820. Daily except Mon., 10-7 and by appointment. Adults, $1; children, 25¢.

Muriel herself greets you at the door leaning on a peppermint-striped cane. After you sign her guest book, you may browse through her assemblage of china, bisque, Parian, wood, wax, apple, tin, celluloid, and fashion dolls reflecting the customs and costumes of their respective eras. There are Indian dolls, Eskimo dolls, Amish dolls, black dolls, and cornhusk, papier-mâché, and rag dolls. The shadow box scenes of an 1886 moonshiner's still, a 1900 barber shop and scenes from Dicken's *Great Expectations* are interesting. Muriel enjoys sharing the stories about her dolls and makes the visit most enjoyable.

The *Wonders of the World Museum* down the block (Fri., Sat. and Sun., 12-5, 25¢) is an off-beat collection of cyclops and sea serpents sculpted out of wood or bones by a man who specializes in dinosaur bones.

THE ALVARADO ADOBE & BLUME HOUSE MUSEUM

1 Alvarado Square, San Pablo. (415) 222-3516. Weekends, 1-5 and by appointment.

The Alvarado Adobe has been precisely reconstructed on its original site. The owner, Juan Bautista Alvarado, husband of Martina Castro, was the Mexican governor of California in 1840, and lived here until 1882. (The house itself was built in the early 1840s for the Castro family.) Although it's still in the process of being furnished in a mix of Rancho and Early California styles, visitors can see a marvelous silver-studded man's hat and suit, showcases of Indian artifacts found in local Indian mounds, *cascarone* balls—painted egg shells that had been filled with confetti or cologne (with which to hit fellow party-goers), an Indian shell game, and samples of the soap plant—*amole*—which was eaten roasted, boiled for glue, pounded into a paste which stupefied fish when thrown into a stream, used for twine, shampoo and soap, and dried to stuff mattresses.

The Blume Museum is a 1920s farmhouse now refurnished to look as it did then, with oak furniture, early plumbing fixtures, and an iron stove in the kitchen.

PUBLIC RELATIONS TOURS

LESLIE SALT COMPANY. 7220 Central Avenue, Newark. (415) 797-1820. Free tours Tues., Wed., and Thurs., 10:30 and 3:30 and by appointment, for children over 8.

See a slide show on how salt is harvested, refined and packaged, then tour the plant to see the pressing, packaging, carton-making, block pressing, and seasoning areas. It's an interesting industrial tour—and also an illuminating one. Did you know that salt is used not only to flavor food and soften water, but also to feed livestock, build roads, and drill oil wells?

HALL OF HEALTH. Alta Bates Hospital, Berkeley. (415) 845-7110 x2447. Mon.–Fri., 10-3 and Sun. 1-4 and by appointment. Free.

Games, displays and exhibits show youngsters how to stay healthy and what hospitals are all about.

KILPATRICK'S BAKERIES. 955 Kennedy, Oakland. (415) 534-3600. Wed. and Thur., 10 and 1 by appointment. Free.

See how bread is baked and packaged.

PARAMOUNT THEATRE OF THE ARTS. 2025 Broadway, Oakland. (415) 465-6400. First Monday of the month at 2; second and fourth Tuesdays at 11, and by appointment. Free.

The Paramount, which has regular programs of interest to children, is the best example of Art Deco architecture on the West Coast. Parquet floors, a gold ceiling teeming with sculptured life, and elegant embellishments almost compete with what's on stage.

GIN SHING BAKERY AND FORTUNE COOKIE FACTORY. 263 12th Street, Oakland. (415) 832-5552. Mon.–Sat., 10-3 and by appointment. Groups, 50¢ per person (everyone gets a bag of cookies).

104

9

SACRAMENTO AND STOCKTON AREA

The Sacramento Area is the political heartland of the state of California. Two hours away from San Francisco, the city of Sacramento is worth a visit to see how the state functions—from the legislative rooms and state displays in the Capitol to the judicial buildings in Capitol Square. The state capital of California has been in Benicia, Vallejo and San Jose. Now, after the one hundredth anniversary of the Capitol building in 1979 and the restoration of the dome, Sacramento seems to be the permanent capital of the State. The green farmland surrounding the city is reflected in the forty-acre Capitol Park within the city, and visitors will appreciate the combination of rural and urban surroundings.

Stockton, south of Sacramento, is the entrance to the Gold Country. Visitors will find the rolling hills and good green farmland dotted by pleasant towns and villages. Stockton is named in honor of Commodore Robert Stockton, who led the forces which took over California for the United States in 1847.

The lakes and peacefulness of the San Joaquin Valley add to the ambience of the area—and water-sports lovers will find ample space for houseboating, skiing, fishing, and every kind of boating.

THE NUT TREE

Nut Tree Road, off Hwy. 80, Vacaville. (707) 448-6411. Daily, 7 a.m.-9 p.m.

The highway signs for the Nut Tree are so pretty you wonder if the restaurant can live up to them. It does. The Nut Tree is much more than a restaurant—it's an afternoon (or morning) of enjoyment. In the restaurant

All aboard—at the California Railway Museum.

itself, three lavishly decorated rooms face huge glass aviaries where brilliantly colored birds fly, sing, and eat fruits and seeds. The lunch menu includes salads, sandwiches, and special lunches priced from $5. Every diner gets an individual loaf of warm bread. Prices are higher at dinner, but you can still order a Dutch plate of cold meats and cheese or a splendiferous fresh fruit plate. Beer is imported from nine countries and the desserts are divine. Children under ten rate a special Train Rider's menu. In the shopping area, a cheese and beer place is comfortable and there are snack bars outside. Free mechanical animals, play mirrors, Polynesian tree huts and funnyface houses will entice the children for hours. Outside the toy store, they can board a miniature train for a five-minute ride (50¢, three for $1). Just think, all this sprung from a single walnut planted by a twelve-year-old girl in 1860.

THE PEÑA ADOBE

5 miles south of Vacaville, on Hwy. 80. Peña Adobe Road. (707) 448-6262. 10-5 daily. Free.

The Peñas and the Vacas were the first Mexican settlers in this area and the Peña adobe is the original one built on an ancient Indian site in the days of the ranchos. It still contains some of the old furnishings and many Wintu Indian artifacts found during restoration. The spool bed and spinning wheel in the bedroom are excellent examples of pioneer craft and the saddles in the bunk room are really worn-out. A small museum tells the story of the first families of the area and of Edwin Markham, the poet, who grew up here. Farm tools and picnic tables are on the grounds.

GLIDERSPORT

Peña Adobe exit, Hwy 80. 10-sunset, weather permitting. (707) 448-4610. Gliding and flying rides and lessons. P.O.B. 176, Vacaville, 95688.

Gliding flights last about fifteen glorious silent minutes ($24 for one; $34 for two) or you can go up for a scenic cruise in a 1928 Travelaire biplane (same price) or the more spectacular aerobatic ride in the Great Lakes replica biplane.
Other soaring centers in Northern California are:
Ames Soaring Club, Patterson Pass Road, Livermore. (415) 447-4110.
Bay Area Soaring Association, 2728 Oak Road, Walnut Creek. (415) 356-9576/984-3045.
Big Valley Soaring, 12145 De Vries Road, Lodi. (209) 466-9820.

Chico Soaring Association, Chico Municipal Airport. (916) 342-6599.

Donner Aviation, Truckee Airport. (916) 587-6559.

North Bay Soaring Club, Sonoma Skypark, San Rafael. (707) 644-0109.

Sacramento Soaring Club, Truckee Airport. (916) 961-8854.

Sky Sailing Airport, Christy Street, Fremont. (415) 651-7671.

Soaring Experience, Inc., Same address as above. (415) 569-2404.

East Bay Soaring Club, 441 San Carlos Way, Novato. (415) 897-4792.

SUTTER'S FORT AND STATE INDIAN MUSEUM STATE HISTORIC PARK

2701 L Street, Sacramento. (916) 445-4209. Daily except holidays, 10-5. Adults, 50¢ (including information wand.); under 18, free (25¢ for information wands). Ticket usable at all state historic parks that day.

Sutter's Fort is one of the best places to relive California history. The fort and its buildings and stables are perfectly reconstructed and the cooperage, distillery, saddle shop, candle-making room, kitchens, trading post, Indian guard room, *vaqueros'* bunk room and Sutter's bachelor and family quarters are all as they once were. The songs and information provided through the wands are clear, helpful and entertaining. While facing a model of James Marshall showing Sutter the gold he found at the mill, you hear their conversation and Sutter's German-Swiss accent. A pioneer lady talks to herself as she bends over the stove, Indians sing while working at shuttle and loom. Live donkeys still stand in the stables and the fire still glows in the blacksmith shop. A small museum relates Sutter's biography and the life of the California pioneers. Our kids were especially taken with the diorama of John Fremont and Kit Carson entering the fort in 1844. The doll that survived the Donner party is also special.

Next to Sutter's Fort, the State Indian Museum (2618 K Street, same hours and phone) houses a fine collection of California Indian relics. The exhibits span archaeology, basketry, featherwork, pottery, maps, minerals, musical instruments, clothing, ceremonies, boats, housing, and jewelry. Did you know that there were over 750 languages spoken by the Indians of North America? Do you know the tribes of Northern California? Here you'll see Maidus grinding acorns, a Mono storage shelter, a Pomo tule boat, a Miwok headdress, a Yokuts dice game, and the ghost dance of the Sioux and Cheyenne. Ishi, last of his California tribe, is here in photographs, starting a fire, skinning a deer, painting, carving, sewing. Other civilizations were here before we were; this place makes you aware of how little we know of them.

CALIFORNIA STATE CAPITOL

Capitol Mall, Sacramento. (916) 445-5200. Free tours from the East Entrance, Mon.–Fri. at 10:30, 1:30 and 2:30 and by appointment.

Visitors may look in on the Assembly and the Senate when the legislature is in session. Fifty-eight displays, one for each county in the state, are on the ground floor of the East Wing. The governor's office is right on the main floor, so you may spot him or some other celebrities.

107

For a different look at the history of California, stop in at the nearby *California State Archives* (1020 O Street, (916) 445-4293, Mon.–Fri., 8-5), to walk through a well-designed exhibit area showing historic documents and pictures.

E. B. CROCKER ART GALLERY

216 O Street, Sacramento. (916) 446-4677. Daily except Mondays and holidays, 10-5; Tues. 2-10 p.m. Free.

The oldest art museum in the West was built around 1873 to house the paintings and prints collected by Judge Edwin Bryant Crocker. The collection now includes pottery from the fifth century B.C. through contemporary works of art. Tile and parquet floors, rococo mirrors, frescoed ceilings, handcrafted woodwork and curving staircases make the building itself a work of art. Concerts, lectures and other special events are scheduled throughout the year.

GOVERNOR'S MANSION

16th and H Streets, Sacramento (916) 445-4209. Tours every half hour from 10 to 4:30 and by appointment daily. Adults, 50¢.

The official residence of California's thirteen governors from 1903 to 1967 is now a handsome Victorian museum that incorporates the history of the state. Living rooms, bedrooms, dining rooms and hallways are furnished in a melange of styles to reflect their different inhabitants. The old carriage house has also been converted to a museum where you may see the hats, fans,

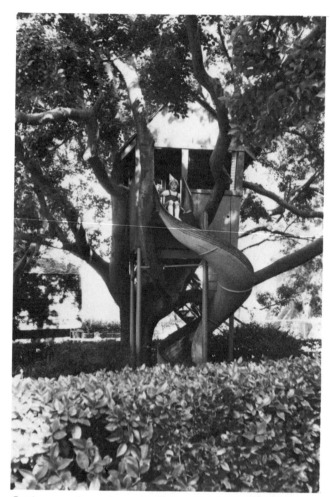

Getting out of a treehouse the fast way in Fairytale Town.

108

Home of the Governors.

parasols and other personal belongings of the governors and their families.

FAIRYTALE TOWN

William Land Park, Sacramento. (916) 449-5233, Tues. – Fri. 10-5; until 6 on summer weekends. Closed December and January. Adults 75¢; children 25¢.

Nursery rhymes and favorite stories all seem quite plausible in this cheerful land of make-believe. Youngsters can crawl through the holes of The Cheese or down The Rabbit's Hole, pet the baby goats at Troll Bridge, see Hiawatha, the Three Little Pigs, the Tortoise, and Mary's Little Lamb. Cinderella's pumpkin coach, King Arthur's Castle, wonderful slides and the Japanese garden, representing a Japanese children's story, complete the array. Just remember: "Please do not sit on the elves."

In the amusement center across the road, carousel and pony rides are available weekends, 11-5, weekdays in summer 11-4:30. Pony rides are 50¢ each, and the other nine rides are 75¢ each.

SACRAMENTO ZOO

3930 West Land Park Drive, Land Park, Sacramento (916) 447-5094. 9-4, daily. Adults $1.50; ages 13-17, 75¢; 6-12, 15¢. (The zoo actually closes at 5 p.m. but the zookeeper thinks his zoo is special enough that it takes at least an hour to enjoy it—so he closes the gates at 4 o'clock, disappointing all those who believe the posted times!)

Almost one thousand animals live in this tree-shaded garden and zoo. The reptile house is a favorite;

109

others are the wallaroos, the flamingos, and the island of monkeys. The river otters have a slide for speedy entry into their pond and the penguins swim smugly in their pool.

OLD SACRAMENTO

Sacramento was the major transportation hub for north-central California, providing a convenient location where water and land transportation systems could meet. Today, along the Sacramento River where Captain John Sutter established his Embarcadero in 1839, an important part of Sacramento's history is being restored to its former glory. Fifty-three structures built during the boom of the Gold Rush stand as living memorials to their past, looking as they did in the 1850s and '60s. Inside are restaurants, stores, offices, and museums. For tour information, call (916) 445-4209.

The Old Eagle Theater at Front and J Streets, opened on October 18, 1849, and now presenting old melodramas and contemporary plays. (Box office information: 446-6761. Tours daily, between 10 and 4. Free.)

The California State Railroad Museum (Front Street, between I and J, 10-5 daily except holidays, 322-3676. Adults 50¢ for State Historic Park ticket) is a reconstruction of a station that existed here in 1876. Waiting rooms, ticket offices, baggage rooms and seven railroad cars tell their stories through tour wands. The star of the show is Lucious Beebe's private car, a glamorously decorated railroad carriage with soft chairs and a fine wooden writing desk.

Old Sacramento Schoolhouse, at Front & L (383-2536), looks just as it did in the 1880s and is open 9:30-4:30, Mon.–Sat., 12-4:30 on Sunday. Free.

B. F. Hastings Museum (Second and J, (445-4655),

10-5, free), was the first western terminus of the Pony Express and the Sacramento office of Wells Fargo. Wells Fargo and Pony Express exhibits fascinate, as do the reconstructed Supreme Court rooms and posters on the early post office system.

Other museums are still under construction, but the bookstores, ice cream and candy stores, fun house of game machines, boutiques, and restaurants make Old Sacramento a full day's adventure. Lady Adams, which houses a cookie and music box store, is the oldest existing building in Old Sacramento, made from materials shipped round the Horn in 1852.

W. G. STONE LOCK

Jefferson Boulevard, at the drawbridge, at the entrance to the port of Sacramento. (916) 371-7540. Visitors overlook open daylight hours. Free.

This one-level six-hundred-foot-long lock connects the Sacramento River to the deep-water ship channel in Sacramento's port for tugs and barges, fishermen and pleasure craft. It takes about fifteen to twenty-five minutes for the water level to raise the ships, depending on the level of the river itself (which is affected by the bay tides) and the locks are worked every half hour or so, depending on water traffic.

FOOD CIRCUS

1735 Arden Way, Arden Fair Shopping Center, Sacramento. (916) 929-4305. Open for breakfast, lunch and dinner.

You want pizza, your spouse yearns for chow mein and the kids are clamoring for hamburgers? You can eat together at Food Circus—twelve restaurants under one roof. Here you can choose from Mexican, Chinese, German, Italian, Japanese, and American standbys, most for under $4.

SACRAMENTO SCIENCE CENTER & JUNIOR MUSEUM

3615 Auburn Boulevard, east area, Sacramento. (916) 485-4471. Mon.–Sat., 9:30-5; Sun. 12-5. Adults 25¢; children 15¢.

Live animals indigenous to California live in the museum, which also offers special films and exhibits, and supervised playtime with the animals on weekends.

SILVER WINGS AVIATION MUSEUM

Mather Air Force Base, Building 3860, Rancho Cordova. (916) 364-2177. 10-4 weekdays, 12-4 weekends. Free.

Military and civilian aircraft displays and fifty-five films dating from the Wright Brothers to Vietnam (shown continuously, by request) are presented in this reproduction of a 1914 hangar. There are World War I and World War II aviation displays, displays on pioneer women, engines and models. The Teeny-Genie, an experimental pleasure plane with a VW engine, is wonderful.

The Mather Planetarium, in Rancho Cordova (916) 364-2908) is open to groups of twelve or more by reservation. You'll see stars, planets, comets, meteor showers, outlines of constellations, and other space phenomena on a domed ceiling.

Aviators who'd rather do than see can contact the

The Teeny-Genie.

River City Balloon Company, 3444 Vougue Court, Sacramento, CA 95826, 362-2000) for balloon flights.

NIMBUS FISH HATCHERY.

2001 Nimbus Road, Rancho Cordoba. (916) 355-0666. Daylight hours, all year. Free.

After fighting their way from the Pacific Ocean, salmon and steelhead spawn here each fall and winter. The hatchery has a capacity of twenty million salmon eggs and accounts for 60 to 70 percent of the commercial catch off the California Coast.

GIBSON RANCH COUNTY PARK.

8552 Gibson Ranch Road, Elverta, (take Watt Avenue north

111

to Elverta Road) (916) 366-2061. Daily, 7 a.m. to dusk. Free.

This 326-acre park is really a working farm. There are cows, hens and horses to feed. Muskrats, ducks and geese swim in the lake, which you can fish. There are ponies and donkeys to ride, paddleboats to rent, old buggies and a blacksmith shop to see, and picnics and hayrides to enjoy. Tours by appointment.

FOLSOM PROJECT DAM AND POWERPLANT

7806 Folsom-Auburn Road, Folsom. (916) 988-1707. 10-2 daily.

Drive on top of the dam, past the gorgeous lake, to get to the powerhouse. Tours pass three generators with capacities of 66,240 kilowatts each, and through the dam, depending upon how many people are visiting at the time.

FOLSOM CITY COMMUNITY PARK AND ZOO

50 Natoma Street, Folsom. (916) 985-3661, x58. 10-4 daily. Donations for food for animals.

Golden eagles, turkey vultures, great horned owls, hawks, and pigeons fly freely in large cages in this "biggest little zoo in the world." Monkeys, coyotes, mountain lions, black bears, lions, tigers and ocelots prance. Deer and ponies graze in a nearby meadow. A perky little train, with a one-third scale live steam engine, runs into the park (50¢).

Historic Sutter Street, in Folsom, is a restored section of old buildings and shops. The miniatures at Dorothea's Peppermint Lane, and Patsy's Soda Parlor take visitors back to gayer times and the Sutter Gaslight Theater, a cider shop and many ethnic restaurants make a short stay worthwhile. At Sutter and Wool Streets, the reconstructed Southern Pacific depot displays historical treasures.

The *Folsom Powerhouse*, on Riley Street, relayed electricity to Sacramento from 1895 to 1952. For tours call (916) 988-0205.

CALIFORNIA RAILWAY MUSEUM

10 miles east of Fairfield on Hwy. 12, Rio Vista Junction. (707) 374-2978. Weekends and holidays, 12-5. Daily in summer. Free entrance to the park and museum. Rides: Adults $1.50, children 75¢ all day.

The California Railway Museum was put together by a non-profit organization of men who love trains. You can walk through and around the more than sixty retired trolleys and steam locomotives or just watch the railroad buffs at work. An old-fashioned Salt Lake & Utah observation car is there for the dreaming (remember Judy Garland and "The Harvey Girls?"), as are Birney Street "dinkeys," an electric cable car, a New York City "El," a Pullman car that's been made up, a Gay Nineties San Francisco street car, a Toonerville Trolley from the Key System, and lots more. The gift shop at the entrance holds the largest collection of railroad books in the West, along with cards, model kits, old ads, tickets, and badges. Picnic areas are available, and rides are frequent on weekends.

RIO VISTA MUSEUM

16 North Front Street, Rio Vista. (707) 374-5169. Weekends, 2-5 and by appointment. Free.

All of the treasures in this little museum have been donated by local residents. There are antique etchings and photos, newspapers and books, and farm implements such as tools, plows, a buggy, a wagon, a forge and a foundry, typewriters, a wine press, Chinese hats, and local birds' eggs. The museum was created during the Bicentennial, "So," says its curator, "we won't forget all about the past."

MICKE GROVE PARK AND ZOO AND SAN JOAQUIN COUNTY HISTORICAL MUSEUM

11793 North Micke Grove Road, 3 miles south of Lodi on Hwy. 99/5. Park phone: (209) 368-4641. Museum: 368-9154. Park hours: dawn to dusk daily, $1 per car on weekends and holidays. Zoo: 10-5 daily. Free. Museum: 10-5 Wed.–Sun. Free.

"Man and Nature Hand in Hand" is the theme of this remarkable multi-building museum created for the Bicentennial. A trotter's sulky greets you at the door of the main building, which focuses on the home. A millinary shop, Victorian sitting room and dining room are meticulously furnished. The exhibits are changed continuously. We saw a beautiful collection of quilts and "Needle/Shuttle & Awl," an interpretation of the techniques employed by Native American women in the manufacture and decoration of items of utilitarian and ceremonial use.

A completely outfitted Liberty Harness shop is on

Tuning in on the past in Old Sacramento.

the grounds as are a ranch blacksmith shop and a school-house that seems to be just waiting for children. One barn concentrates on the grapes, fruits and nuts produced in the area; another focuses on the River Delta, the Indians of the marshland, and the conquering of water and soil. "Earth is here so kind, that just tickle her with a hoe and she laughs up a harvest," is what one Delta farmer wrote. A large building filled with plows, hoes, wagons, forks, axes, and farm implements of every other kind shows how the harvesting was—and is still—done.

Lions, bobcats, green monkeys, grey foxes, kinka-jous, pumas and black leopards are some of the animals in the nice little zoo. There are public feedings of the birds and animals at one o'clock every day.

Picnic areas, an amusement park with lots of kiddie rides, a swimming pool, and peaceful rose and Japanese gardens add to the attraction of this pleasant park.

POLLARDVILLE GHOST TOWN

10464 Hwy 99/5, 3 miles above Stockton. (209) 931-0272/4571. Weekends, 12-5:30. Adults $1.50, chil-dren and seniors, 75¢.

Pollardville Ghost Town is made up of both movie set and real buildings brought down from the Mother Lode country. The Jamestown Jail was brought from Calaveras County and the Freedom Gazette newspaper building from Jackson. The hotel starred in Gregory Peck's "Big Country." Gunfights are staged and you can ride the Rock & Roll Railroad as it barrels around town on its regular runs (50¢). Visitors can see an 1880s livery stable, a dentist's and doctor's office, and an undertaker's establishment. Vaudeville and melodrama are present at

the old Palace Theater on weekends in the summer. The Chicken Kitchen, at the entrance, dispenses chicken dinners in an Old West atmosphere.

PIONEER MUSEUM AND HAGGIN GALLERIES

1201 North Pershing Avenue, Victory Park, Stockton. (209) 462-4116. 1:30-5 daily except Mondays and holidays. Free.

Three floors of history and art fill this handsome brick building. Interpretive displays of California and local history include an arcade of nineteenth century storefronts, arms and mining lamps and vehicle galleries, and an Indian Room. There are fossils and geological displays and memorabilia of Stockton's past, and a gor-geous green and red harvesting machine. The art galleries include works by Old Masters and California artists such as Albert Bierstadt. Our kids honed in on the letter by Daniel Boone, the Donner party relics, the port diorama, and the display of one hundred years of dolls.

PIXIE WOODS

Louis Park, Stockton. (209) 466-9890/944-8220. Fall and spring weekends, 12-6; Wed.–Fri. 11-6 and weekends 12-7 in summer. Closed from right after Thanksgiving to Easter Week. Over 12: 30¢; under: 25¢. Train and boat rides: 30¢; Merry-go-round 20¢.

When you enter the rainbow gate of Pixie Woods, you enter a children's fairyland built entirely by the people of Stockton. Children can play in a castle, on a pirate ship, around a rocket ship, and on a fire engine. They can ride on a Chinese dragon and slide down a colored slide, and talk to Little Miss Muffet. The volcano erupts regularly in Pirate's Cove. At MacGregor's Farm, you can pet pigs, sheep, rabbits, and Billy Goats Gruff. You can even have parties with Alice in Wonderland.

MILLER HORSE AND BUGGY RANCH

9425 Yosemite Boulevard at Hwy. 132, Modesto. (209) 522-1781. Open "whenever Mrs. Mae Miller is there, which is most of the time." Adults, $1; children under 12, 50¢.

This wagon collection and 1900 general store are absolutely fascinating, but they are so cluttered that some people may shy away. Those who climb in and poke around will be well-rewarded. Over fifty cars and wagons, including stage coaches, fire engines, beer wagons, racing sulkies, Victoria coaches, excursion buses, and an ambulance used in the San Francisco earthquake are in the barn. A hurdy-gurdy and high-button shoes, sausage stuffers, old typewriters, and a bicycle collection dating to the 1820s (including a mother-of-pearl tandem bike reputedly given to Lillian Russell by "Diamond Jim" Brady) are in the store.

In Modesto proper is a new Victorian museum, *The McHenry Mansion* (1402 I Street, 577-5366, 12-4 except Mon. Free) is being put together. You'll see gold mining artifacts, World War I relics, old fashioned rooms, and more.

PUBLIC RELATIONS TOURS

CALIFORNIA ALMOND GROWERS EXCHANGE. 18th and C Streets, Sacramento. (916) 442-6771. Mon.–Fri., 10, 1, and 2. Sat. Movie only at 11 & 3. Free. Groups by appointment.

Franciscan fathers brought the almond from Spain to California in 1769. Today, Blue Diamond is the world's largest almond packer. Visitors see many unusual machines designed to sort, crack, halve, slice, and dice roasted almonds. You see concrete bins eight stories high, a mile-long conveyor belt, and an explanatory movie on the hour-long tour. Then dig into the ten different flavored almonds in the tasting room (open 8-5:30 weekdays, 10-4 Saturday). An authentic London red double-decker bus takes Old Sacramento visitors to the plant three times a day during the week.

HERSHEY FOODS

1400 Albers Road, Oakdale. (209) 847-0381. Mon.–Fri. 8:15-3 by appointment. Free.

Candy bars, chocolate kisses, and chocolate syrups are made, weighed, packaged and labeled in the course of this thirty-minute tour. You pass huge chocolate vats, candy-bar molds in action, and rooms for the processing of instant cocoa and chocolate syrup. Every visitor gets a free candy bar!

10

THE GOLD COUNTRY

To drive along Highway 49 is to experience California's colorful history and legends. This is the Gold Country — the land of writers like Mark Twain, Bret Harte and Joaquin Miller, bandits like Black Bart and Joaquin Murietta, and heroes like Ulysses S. Grant and Horatio Alger. Passing through little towns named Copperopolis and Jenny Lind, visitors who look carefully will see the traces of the hundreds of thousands of people — Cornish, Welsh, English, German, French, Italian, Mexican, Peruvian, Australian, Chinese and African — who migrated to this place seeking fame and fortune. The town of Volcano still has an old Chinese store and a Jewish cemetery. The many parks and campgrounds are inevitably near quiet streams that once teemed with gold panners. In Gold Country you'll find the only town in the United States ever to name itself a nation: Rough and Ready seceded from the Union on April 7, 1850 to become a republic with its own president, constitution and flag. (By July 4th, it had slipped quietly back into the United States.) The best thing to do in the Gold Country is just explore and talk to the natives; you'll have good experiences that you couldn't possibly find listed in a book and you'll hear about towns that exist now only in memory.

RAIL TOWN 1897 & THE SIERRA RAILROAD COMPANY

Off Highways 49 and 108 on Fifth Ave., Jamestown. (209) 984-3953. 9-5 daily in summer, and weekends, fall and spring. Roundhouse tours $1.55, over 16; 70¢, 5-15.
   Varying prices for special train rides, twilight

cruises and weekend excursions by rail, starting at $5.75 for adults, $2 for ages 5-15 (including roundhouse tour). The future of the Sierra Railroad was in doubt at press time, so do call before starting out.

The Sierra's Mother Lode Cannonball steam engine speeds for an hour through the Mother Lode to the town of Chinese Camp or into tall pine woods to Fassler. At the station, you'll see a working blacksmith shop, wood shop, car repair shops, a machine shop still powered by belts, the turntable, and the roundhouse. The locomotives here appear in movies frequently, so you may recognize them. We saw an old green engine loaded with wood ready for its role in the new Jesse James movie. For tickets and information: Sierra R.R. Drawer 515, Jamestown, 95327 (in San Francisco call 398-3178).

TUOLUMNE COUNTY HISTORICAL MUSEUM

158 W. Bradford, Sonora. (209) 532-4212. 9-12 and 1-5, Mon.–Fri., 10-3 weekends in summer. Free.

The 1866 brick jail now serves as a small but thriving museum of the Gold Country. A Yosemite bear gun and foot warmer for the stage coach drivers are our favorite things to see here. Our favorite thing to do is to take a walk through the town of Sonora, once called "the Queen of the Southern Mines."

WESTSIDE & CHERRY VALLEY RAILWAY

Tuolumne-Sonora Road, Tuolumne City. (209) 928-4282. 10-10 daily in summer, 10-5 weekends in winter, weather permitting.

The old West Side Flume and Lumber Company is being converted into 260 acres of park and museum. There are train rides, railcar tours, walking tours, Mexican excursion boat rides, and antique vehicle rides, priced from $1 to $6 for adults for all five. Or you can simply wander through on your own, through the depot kitchen and the Mexican Village, looking at the old cars and trucks and logging equipment on the grounds. A "country village" is next on the agenda for this welcoming park, which will take another five years to complete.

COLUMBIA STATE HISTORIC PARK

Hwy. 49, Columbia. (209) 532-4301. 9-5 daily, except holidays. Free.

Columbia, "The Gem of the Southern Mines," is a restored goldmining town of the 1850s. The streets and wooden sidewalks lead you to buildings, stores and eateries outfitted as they were in the town's heyday. The Columbia Gazette office, open to the public on weekends and all summer, still prints a small newspaper; the Columbia Candy Kitchen still sells hand-dipped penny candy; the 1857 Douglas Saloon still dispenses an occasional draft along with the sarsasparilla. Peek into the carpenter's shop, the ice depot and the schoolhouse, which is furnished with bell tower, pump organ, desks and potbellied stoves. The Chinese herb shop, the fandango hall and the town jail and drugstore are all Main Street attractions. Fallon House, which once starred Lola Montez and Edwin Booth, has a summer repertory company. The gold scales in the Wells Fargo office weighed out over $55 million in dust and nuggets of the $87,000,000 mined here. At the Hidden Treasure Gold Mine Tour (532-9693, $5 for adults, $2.50 for children) you can try your hand at panning yourself. The park museum offers exhibits on the Indians, the Chinese population (once one-sixth of Columbia) and, of course, the gold miners. The collection of old dolls and toys is noteworthy. Picnic spots are available, so plan to spend an enjoyable day in this thriving town of yesteryear.

MOANING CAVE

Vallecito, on the road between Columbia State Historic Park and Hwy. 4, (209) 736-2708. Open 9-6 daily in summer and on weekends in winter, 10-5 winter weekdays, closed Christmas. Adults $3; under 11, $1.50.

You can count the 144 winding steps that lead you 165 feet down to a graveyard of prehistoric bones and moaning winds. You'll see fantastic rock formations, such as Elephant's Ears and the Little Girl's Face, that add to the eerie feeling that you're intruding on unknown spirits. The main chamber is large enough to hold the Statue of Liberty. Picnic tables and a view of the hills offer a pleasant waiting space, as does the exhibit filled waiting room. Stalactites hang "tight" from the ceiling and stalagmites are "mighty mounds" on the floor— that's how we remember which is which.

OLD TIMERS MUSEUM

Main Street, Murphys. 10-5 winter weekends and Wed. – Sun. in summer. 25¢.

An old time bedroom, bar, furnished blacksmith shop, portrait of J. Pierpont Morgan and an antique bicycle are the highpoints of this old-fashioned assemblage of gold-mining memories.

Down the block, *The Peppermint Stick* (728-3570) entices with old-fashioned sodas and sundaes, creations such as "Claim Jumpers" and the "Pick and Shovel Special" and peppermint ice cream cones for travelers on the run.

MERCER CAVERNS

Ebbetts Pass Hwy., 1 mile from Murphys. (209) 728-2101. 9-5 daily in summer; 11-4 winter weekends and holidays. Adults $2.75; 5-11 $1.25.

This thirty-minute tour past stalactites and stalagmites, aragonites and helictites takes you into a subterranean wonderland. Eerie rock formations like the Organ Loft, Angel Wings and the Chinese Meat Market are dazzling examples of the artistry of nature. Mercer Caverns was discovered in 1885 by a tired, thirsty prospector, Walter J. Mercer, who noticed bay bushes growing near a limestone bluff and thought he had found water.

ANGELS CAMP MUSEUM

753 Main Street, Angels Camp, on Hwy. 49. (209) 736-2963. 9-4:30 daily in summer; 11-4 except Tues. and Wed. in winter. Adults 50¢, 6-12 25¢.

A mortician's embalming kit and hearse, models of a stamp mill and the Wild Goose Mine, a cheese press and a waffle iron, minerals, gemstones and hunks of quartz containing gold are the main attractions in this cluttered museum. A rusty old fire engine, petrified wood, cave stalactites and exotic old mining machines surround the building.

If you stay on Hwy. 49 between Columbia and Angels Camp, you may want to stop for a peak into a replica of *Mark Twain's Cabin* on Jackass Hill. Here he gathered material for his *Jumping Frog of Calaveras County* and wrote *Roughing It* — this was a turning point in his career.

CALAVERAS COUNTY HISTORICAL MUSEUM

Main Street, San Andreas. (209) 754-4203. 10-4 daily. Courthouse tours at 11, 1 and 3 and by appointment. 50¢ adults; 25¢ children.

The Calaveras County Courthouse and County Jail of 1867 has been transformed into a beautifully designed treasure house. You can walk through the judge's chambers (where the judge's robe still hangs) and then go downstairs to see the cell where Black Bart awaited trial. The Comanche Catholic Church is inside a huge safe. Local hero Pete Orme's jockey silks are on one wall and there's a large exhibit of Miwok Indian artifacts. The representative bedroom and parlor, miner's cabin and general store are extremely well-done and well-labeled. Much of the work on the County Courthouse was done as a Bicentennial project.

AMADOR COUNTY MUSEUM

225 Church Street, Jackson. (209) 223-2884. Thurs. – Mon. 11:30-4. Adults $1; children 50¢.

Working models, built to a scale of one and one-half inch to the foot, using original materials, of the North Star Mine stamp, the Kennedy Mine Tailing Wheel No. 2 and the Kennedy Mine head frame are demonstrated regularly on weekends and by appointment. The museum collection also includes a wooden bathtub, musical and medical instruments, an oak chest

Down the stairs to Mercer Caverns' fantasy world.

120

used to carry water on an 1852 covered wagon and a folding chair and foot-operated drill used by a traveling dentist.

One mile out North Main Street, there are two wheels on each side of the road, fifty-eight feet in diameter. They were used to transport waste from the mine. The *Jackson Trailing Wheels* are almost lost in history, but their size is still impressive.

CHAW-SE INDIAN GRINDING ROCK STATE HISTORIC PARK

Pine Grove-Volcano Road, Volcano. (209) 296-4440. Daily, weather permitting. Day use per car: $2.

When you walk up to the top of the hill, all you see is a huge, flat rock with a few pockmarks and scratchy lines, surrounded by a wooden fence. Then you get closer and see that the scratchy lines are petroglyphs by the Miwok Indians to commemorate their tales of hunting and fishing. The pockmarks are actually mortar holes—1,185 of them—in which the Indian women ground the seeds, bulbs, fungi and acorns that served as the staples of their diet. Each of the mortar holes was abandoned when it became too deep. The acorn meal was sifted and washed many times to remove bitterness, then the meal was mixed with water in a basket, and heated by hot rocks dropped into the mush. One family consumed two thousand pounds of acorn a year. An extensive Indian Cultural Center and Museum, incorporating Miwok bark houses, a ceremonial roundhouse and corn granary is now being built. The center offers interpretive information, classes in Indian crafts, and Miwok Indians participating in the sharing of the Indian spirit.

In Volcano itself, *The Jug and Rose Confectionary Shop* has been serving breakfasts, lunches and sweets garnished with fresh flowers since 1855. Prices are modest and children are made especially welcome at their own small table.

CHEW KEE STORE

Fiddletown. Just off Hwy. 49, out of Plymouth.

Built in the 1850s, the Chew Kee Store is believed to be California's only surviving rammed-earth structure of the Gold Rush era and has been called "a truly remarkable showcase for history frozen in time." A small shrine, a lantern made from a five-gallon oil can, ceramic rice crocks, pipes, brass opium cans, food safes, gambling hall receipts, a long black queue in a glass display case and the full stock of a Chinese herb store will soon be on view as the store becomes part of the state parks system.

SAM'S TOWN AMERICANA MUSEUM

Cameron Park, Hwy. 80, Shingle Springs. (916) 933-1662/677-2273. Open from 9:30-6:30 daily; longer hours in summer and on weekends. 50¢ adults; 25¢ children.

Sam's is a town, restaurant, and amusement park all in one. The front of the building looks like an old town, with doctor's office, stable, saloon, and theater, but inside it is one large building divided into restaurants, a gift and book shop, a honky-tonk piano bar, a fun arcade, and the *Americana Museum*. Thirty scenes portray fine old times from the days of the steam horse-drawn fire engine, to Jenny Lind and Lillian Russell in concert, to old Saturday Night Bath Time. Vintage vehicles— paddy wagons, trolley cars, buggies, surreys and chariots—stand on the grounds.

EL DORADO COUNTY HISTORICAL MUSEUM

El Dorado County Fairgrounds, Placerville. (916) 626-2250. 10-4 Wed.–Sat; 12-3:30 Sun. Free.

Gold mining and history of the farming pioneers are focal points for this relatively new collection. A seed broadcaster mounted on a Spring wagon and pulled by horses, a mammoth universal concentrator, or shaking table, on flexible legs (it could separate the gold from one-and-a-half tons of mercury hardrock ore per hour), and a walk-in Shay engine #4, once used to pull logs and equipment grabbed the kids' attention here.

GOLD BUG MINE

Bedford Park, Placerville. (916) 622-0832. 8:30- 4:30 daily. Free.

The only municipally owned, open-to-the-public gold mine in the world was worked as recently as 1947. The longer shaft of the mine ends at an exposed gold-bearing quartz vein. The occasional drip of water rings in the cool, eerie silence of the tunnel. The huge gold-stamp mill by the creek is still undergoing restoration.

Placerville itself was called Old Hangtown, after the Hanging Tree in the center of town. A walk through the town, from the Pony Express Harness Shop at 3030 Sacramento, which used to be the Western Terminus of the Pony Express in 1861, to the Wells Fargo Office, once the scene of busy gold shipments, will illustrate its history.

East on Highway 50, the *Camino Narrow Gauge Railway* runs on weekends from 11 to 5. *The Michigan-California Lumber Company* nearby arranges tours which begin with uncut logs and end with lumber being loaded into freight cars.

GHOST MOUNTAIN

Pollack Pines. Hwy. 50 above Placerville. (916) 644-2415. Daily in summer, weekends in winter, weather permitting.

Day visitors to this campground can stroll through a Wells Fargo Office, the jail, the general store, the Indian village and museum, an old-time hotel and chapel, ride a pony or stagecoach, and join in a Western barbecue. A complete ghost town is being rebuilt in which every building will house a working craftsman to show you what life was like in Gold Rush days.

MARSHALL GOLD DISCOVERY STATE
HISTORIC PARK

Hwy. 49, Coloma (916) 622-3470. 10-5 daily except holidays. Adult state parks ticket, 50¢. Camping/pic-

Boy and stagecoach in Marshall Gold Discovery SHP.

nicking $1.50 per car.

Sutter's Mill has risen again on the American River. The museum is modern—a complete exhibit of the discovery of gold and the lives of the gold miners. There are maps, tools and mementos of the miners, a pictorial display of the discovery, an exhibit of the Gold Rush routes and a piece of timber from the first mill. Gold dust and nuggets, geological exhibits and the story of the Maidu Indians are also displayed, along with the diary of miner F. C. Negler and dioramas of history. There are Gold Rush films on weekends. On the grounds, an 1860 general store and bank, a Chinese store, and a stamp mill are equipped and in working order. The table in the Mormon workers' cabin is set for dinner. The miner's cabin is furnished with a tin of coffee, cans of beans, a scale, a Bible, and the miner himself, in bed with his boots on. The blacksmith shop, gunsmith shop, arrastre (ore crusher), and hydraulic mining displays are also of interest. But the best thing of all is to stand next to the big wheel of the mill and look at this quiet spot that changed history. The ranger has been known to saw a log or two in the mill on weekends.

Right next to the park, the *Sierra Nevada House III* (Coloma, Hwy. 49, (916) 622-5856) has been offering meals, snacks, rooms, and ice cream confections in its various incarnations ever since 1850. There's even a gigantic gold-weighing scale in the main dining room.

PLACER COUNTY HISTORICAL MUSEUM

Gold Country Fairgrounds, 1273 High Street, Auburn, (916) 885-9570. Mon.–Fri. 10-4; until 5 on weekends. Free.

Old mining equipment and pioneer mementos depict the early days of Placer County. The colorful calliope and stained-glass model of the County courthouse and the wishing well are special favorites. Birds nests, blackjacks, an olive press, and the wooden washing machine in the replica kitchen also drew comment. Local school children can participate in the Living History programs that include gold-panning lessons and tasting Indian acorn soup.

In nearby Old Town, antique shops and an old-fashioned tower firehouse are open for inspection.

NORTH STAR MINE POWERHOUSE MUSEUM

Lower Mill Street, at Empire. Grass Valley. (916) 273-9853. 11-5 daily in summer, 10-4 except Wed. and Thurs. in winter. Adult ticket 50¢.

Built by A. D. Foote in 1875, this is the first completely water-powered compressed-air transmission plant of its kind. The compressed air, generated by ten-ton, thirty-foot Pelton water wheels, furnished power for the entire mine. The museum houses photos, ore specimens, enticing safes, mining dioramas, models of mines, an assaying laboratory, carbide lamps and "widowmaker" drill bits, but the main attractions are the wheels, suspension bridges and walkways of the building itself.

Down the block, the *Grass Valley Museum in Mount St. Mary's* (on South Church, 12-3 daily except holidays, 50¢) offers vintage furnishings including an 1880s doctor's office, a school room, children's bedrooms, and convent artifacts, such as the silver press used for making the Host.

Further along on Mill Street are the homes of Lola Montez and Lotta Crabtree. Lola was a Bavarian singer, dancer and king's favorite who fled to America in 1853 when her king fell from power. Lotta Crabtree became Lola's protégé and soon became famous, rich, and beloved by the American public. Lola's home is open to the public daily (12-4, free), in the summer.

EMPIRE MINE STATE HISTORIC PARK

Ophir Hill, Central Park, Grass Valley. (916) 273-8522. 9-5 daily except holidays; tours by appointment. Adult parks ticket, 50¢.

Telling the story of hard-rock gold mining and its significance in California's history, the Empire is the oldest, largest, and richest gold mine in the area. Many of the sixteen stopping points along the mine's self-guiding tour are in ruins or the events exist only in memory and the sites are being reconstructed. Movies shown on weekends help excite your imagination. "Gone are the hundreds of Cornish miners who dug the 367 miles of tunnels to a depth of nearly 12,000 feet on the incline, over a mile below the surface; gone are the hoists that lowered the men the thousands of feet down the shaft; gone are the mules that pulled the ore trains through the tunnels. But the gold is still there, awaiting a time when mining it will again be profitable."

NEVADA COUNTY HISTORICAL SOCIETY MUSEUMS

Firehouse No. 1, Main and Commercial Streets, Nevada City. (916) 265-9941, 11-5 except holidays. Donation. Bicentennial Museum, foot of Commercial Street, 1-4 except Mondays and holidays. Donation. Tours by appointment (273-9874).

The most frequently photographed item in the firehouse is a photographic portrait of an early mine owner whose own image as a twelve-year-old boy mysteriously appeared at his left shoulder when the photographer developed the negative more than ninety years ago. Other spirits supposedly rearrange the exhibits at night and prod visitors by day. A glowing Chinese altar, Maidu artifacts, relics of the Donner party, children's toys and books and pioneer mementos fill this museum to overflowing. The Bicentennial Museum, or annex, takes up the overflow with a strange collection of robes from local fraternal organizations, sleighbells, and other oddities.

The American Victorian Museum (325 Spring Street, 265-5804, 9:30-4 (except Tues.) and during dinner. Free.) occupies the 1856 Miners Foundry, which manufactured the famous Pelton water wheel. The museum collects, preserves, and exhibits artifacts of the Victorian Era including an 1887 Dutch Street organ, an 1871 pipe organ and a 1913 theater organ, plus graphics, paintings, games, and toys. Meals are served in the uniquely decorated Foundry room and repertory theater is offered on weekends. Museum personnel can also show you the 1873 *Martin Luther Marsh House*, a Victorian Italianate residence at 254 Boulder Street, with guided tours at 1 and 2:15 weekends, and by appointment (except in winter).

MALAKOFF DIGGINS STATE HISTORIC PARK

North Bloomfield. 17 miles NE of Nevada City on a crooked mountain road. (916) 265-2740. 10-5 daily in summer, weekends in fall and spring. Free.

Many millions of dollar's worth of gold poured from these huge hydraulic diggings, and a small sign informs visitors that there's still enough gold left here, and on other sites throughout the Gold Country, to mine $12 million worth annually for the next fifty years. The museum displays a model of the monitor used in the gold mines, showing how hydraulic mining worked. Photos of the two-mile Bloomfield tunnel, the twelve-foot-long skis used by miners, a portable undertaker's table, mementos of the Chinese miners and an old-time bar and poker room are some of the highlights. Other buildings and the gold mine itself can be seen on walking tours.

SIERRA COUNTY MUSEUM

Main Street, Downieville. 9:30-4 daily, in summer and by appointment. Free.

Keepsakes of the hardy pioneers of Downieville are housed in this old stone building. Outside is a scale model of an arrastre from the Sierra Buttes Mine that crushed ore more finely than the tailings from a stamp mill, along with a hand-operated hundred-year-old valve used to control water pressure in the early hydraulic diggings at Morristown.

KENTUCKY MINE MUSEUM

Hwy. 49, Sierra City. (916) 862-1310. 10-5 Wed.–Sun.

Daily mid-June to mid-September and weekends when weather permits, and by appointment. Tour: $1 for adults, under 12 free. Museum: 50¢ for adults.

A five-stamp mill built in the 1870s, an 1888 ten-stamp mill and a hard rock gold mine are shown during a fascinating forty-minute tour. The Ranch Room traces logging "from team to steam" and displays Indian artifacts, a Victorian wicker baby carriage, an organ, a Chinese doll, and other artifacts, and a wonderful collection of Depression glass.

PLUMAS-EUREKA STATE PARK MUSEUM

Off Hwy. 89, Johnsville. (916) 836-2380. Daily 8-5 in summer; until 4:30 spring and fall. Closed holidays. Free.

Snowshoe Thompson used to carry sixty to eighty pounds of mail on his back over the Sierra in winter for the miners. A pair of his skis are presented in this fully packed museum, along with hardrock mining displays, an assay office, models of a stamp mill and an arrestre, natural history exhibits and pioneer life exhibits.

DONNER MEMORIAL STATE PARK

Donner Lake, Truckee. (916) 587-3789. Daily 9-5 in summer, 10-12 and 1-4 winter weekends, weather permitting. 50¢.

The Emigrant Trail museum combines natural history with one of the most dramatic of human stories. Man's conquest of the Sierra Nevada and the tragic story of the Donner party are told with relics, dioramas, pictures, and models. During the disastrous winter of 1846, a party of 189 tried to make it to California. Only forty-seven people survived. The memorial to the Donner Party is twenty-two feet high, symbolic of the twenty-two foot early snowfall that trapped them. Chinese railroad workers, the "Big Four" railroad tycoons, miners and mountain men are also remembered here.

LAKE TAHOE

Visitors Center, Hwy. 89. South Lake Tahoe. (916) 541-0209/544-5050. Road conditions: (800) 822-5977.

Lake Tahoe is world-famous for its crystal-clear water and beautiful surroundings. Visitors can ski, water-ski, boat, swim (but only in August unless you're a polar bear), sun, backpack and hike, or just enjoy the forest wilderness. Naturalist programs are given on summer weekends in the D. L. Bliss and Emerald Bay State Parks and at Camp Richardson. Movies and shows are held in the Lake of the Sky Amphitheater. Tahoe Cruises, boats and sea-plane rides are also available. (525-7143/546-3185). If you can, take a cruise on the *M.S. Dixie Paddlewheeler* (702) 588-3508. The boat is berthed at Zephyr Cove, eight miles north of Stateline.

The *Boreal Alpine Slide* is a new Lake Tahoe adventure that combines bob-sledding and tray-sliding and is open from 10 to 10 daily in summer, weekends in winter. A chairlift lifts you to the top of Boreal Mountain (ten miles west of Truckee on Hwy. 80) and you swoosh down three thousand feet of straight-aways, curves and banked turns.

Vikingsholm, a thirty-eight-room Nordic fortress, is open to the public from 10 to 5 daily, in summer, on Emerald Bay's southwest shore.

The Lake Tahoe Historical Society Log Cabin Museum on Star Lake Avenue behind the fire station (10-4 daily in summer) features artifacts from Lake Tahoe's earliest days. The Gatekeeper's Log House (located at the outlet for the lake which is the headwaters of the Truckee River), is being restored on Hwy. 89 in Tahoe City as a museum. And the Ehrmann Mansion and the preserved cabin of General Phipps, one of Tahoe's first settlers, are being opened to the public in Sugarpine Point State Park.

The *Taylor Creek Stream Profile Chamber* (daily in summer, 9-5, Wed.—Sun., 10-4 in fall) near Camp Richardson is part of the El Dorado National Forest Visitors Center. You can take one of their self-guided nature walks through a mountain meadow and marsh and down into the chamber, where you look through glass windows to see the rainbow trout and aquatic life of a naturally flowing mountain stream. Recorded messages help you identify the fish and plants in front of you.

You may want to venture to the Nevada side of the lake for a visit to the *Ponderosa Ranch* (Incline Village. 702/831-0691; 10-6 daily in summer and weekends in early fall and late spring; $3 adults; $1.50 children) to

Heavenly Valley—South Lake Tahoe.

see the Cartwright Ranch House, Hoss's Mystery Mine, Frontier Town, an antique car and carriage museum, the Ponderosa barnyard, and other rides and attractions on this television-film set.

But you'll always head back to that glorious lake, named in the language of the Washoe Tribe "Big Water," gouged from the crown of the Sierra during the Ice Age.

11

THE FRESNO AREA

Some people think that Fresno exists only as a stopping off place from San Francisco to Los Angeles, but it's actually a big, booming city in its own right, with lots of good Armenian restaurants and a beautiful city park. The trip to Fresno is a good, long four hours by car from San Francisco, but there are so many motels in the city you can usually be assured of a room when you arrive. Surrounded by rich farm-land, pretty lakes and an impressive irrigation system, Fresno is also the entrance to Sierra National Forest and Sequoia, Kings Canyon, and Yosemite National Parks.

R. C. BAKER MEMORIAL MUSEUM

297 West Elm, Coalinga. (209) 935-1914. Mon.–Fri. 9-12, 1-5; Sat. 11-5; Sun. 1-5. Free.
The newly remodeled R. C. Baker Museum, named in honor of a Coalinga pioneer, oilman and inventor, shows both the natural and "man-made" history of Coalinga. The land surrounding Coalinga is rich with oil and minerals and the museum emphasizes these assets. The oil is also responsible for the numerous well-preserved fossils found near here, including mastadon skeletons and an oil-preserved primeval lizard. Artifacts of the first men to live here, the Tachi tribe of the Yokut nation, include evidence that they used oil for trading. The crowded 1910 kitchen, 1880 advertising cards, collection of porcelain and glass insulators for telephone poles, and the doll collection are fascinating. Two of the most unusual treasures are six hundred kinds of barbed

wire dating from 1867 and a 1908 quilt made of silk swatches that were packed in Nebo cigarettes. There's even a "surrey with the fringe on top." The back room holds tools and machinery used in the oil fields.

Visitors to Coalinga will enjoy a drive nine miles north on Highways 33 and 198 past the Grasshopper oil pumps—oil field characters painted in many colors to look like clowns, birds and animals.

TULARE COUNTY MUSEUM

Mooney Grove Park, Visalia. (209) 733-6613. Daily, 10-4; closed Tues. and Wed. in winter. Closed Tues. in summer. 50¢ (school groups free).

"End of the Trail," the bronz sculpture by James Earl Fraser portraying a tired Indian on a pony—once the most copied piece of art in the world—is the star attraction at this lively museum, which was once a jail house. That sculpture, and "Pioneer" another by Fraser, were first exhibited in San Francisco in 1915 at the Pan-Pacific Exposition. A one-room school house, newspaper and dental office and rooms from turn-of-the-century homes recreate the past. Furniture, clothes, cooking utensils, toys, baskets, World War I uniforms and early farm machinery are also exhibited.

Outside, the 143-acre park offers picnic arbors under oak trees, free boating, skateboard tracks, and more.

THE DEPOT RESTAURANT

207 E. Oak Street, Railway Square, Visalia. (209) 732-8611. Lunch 11-2:30; dinner 5-10, until 11 on Fri. and Sat.; Sun. 4-9:30.

The old Visalia train station across the street from the museum is now a handsome restaurant with a railroad motif. The lunch menu, in the shape of an engine, offers "Pullman Pleaser" and "Brass-Pounder" burgers along with salads and sandwiches. At dinner, the "Caboose Special" (prime rib) and "Engineer's Delight" (steak and lobster) headline the bill.

LINDSAY OLIVE GROWERS

620 N. Westwood, Lindsay. (209) 562-5121. Mon.—Fri. 9-11 and 1-4. Plant closed May through Aug. Tours every hour and by appointment.

Do your kids like olives? If so, they'll love this tasting and learning experience. In the hour walk through the plant, visitors learn the history of olive growing in California and the processing and packaging of this delicious fruit. The olives are washed down sluices of California redwood into a barrel of brine for aging and then cooked for seven days in bubbling salt water until they're black and shiny. The tasting room offers relishes and pimento-filled, black and ripe green olives. When we were there, a class of fourth-graders descended and finished everything on the tasting table in three minutes flat.

PORTERVILLE MUSEUM

257 North D Street, Porterville. (209) 784-9711. Thurs.—Sat., 10-5. Free.

The old Southern Pacific Railroad Station is now an interesting accumulation of historical artifacts of the Porterville pioneers. An original land grant certificate, an 1890s wedding dress, an 1870s corn-sheller, and old dolls are in the main room. Typewriters, early office machines, furniture, and the first switchboard of the Porterville hotel are in back rooms. There are also Indian blankets, baskets and beadwork, and stuffed animals indigenous to the county—a California condor, a golden eagle, mountain lions, bay lynx and birds. (By the way, we actually saw one of the rare, vile-looking condors on the road to Porterville.) The complete turn-of-the-century pharmacy makes you wonder how anyone managed to stay healthy. Fire wagons, covered wagons and farming, carpenter and mining tools are on the grounds. A gracious lady, who knows all about Porterville's first families, enjoys telling the stories behind the treasures over which she presides.

COL. ALLENSWORTH STATE HISTORIC PARK

Twenty miles north of Wasco on Hwy. 43, and nine miles west of Earlimart on Hwy. 99. Sotourna Avenue, Allensworth. (805) 849-3433.

The only California town to be founded, financed and governed by Black Americans is being restored to its 1908 state. A museum dealing with Black culture and history and Colonel Allensworth's home are almost finished.

SUN MAID RAISIN GROWERS

1325 South Bethel Avenue, off old Hwy. 99, Kingsburg. (209) 897-5961. Tours by appointment. Free.

Children of all ages are made most welcome here.

Hostesses in the Sun Maid costumes escort tours that end in the sample room. Visitors are also given samples to take home.

DISCOVERY CENTER

1944 North Winery Avenue, Fresno. (209) 251-5531. Tues.–Sat., 9-5; Sun. 12-5. Adults $1; ages 6-17 50¢. Group rates. Astronomy program in summer.

This hands-on science center helps children try out things for themselves. There's a bubble machine, a chromium mirror, a tree that lights up by sound, a feel box, a reaction machine, and a peripheral-vision tester. The Indian room has a one-hundred-year-old Yokut hut and shows the many things that the Indian has introduced to civilization such as tobacco, lacrosse, snowshoes, dyes, cranberries, pumpkins, turkey, cashews, and tomatoes. Dioramas of lake and valley birds are accompanied by questions to help you learn.

FORESTIERE UNDERGROUND GARDENS

5201 W. Shaw Avenue (at Freeway 99), Fresno. (209) 485-3281. Tours every hour on the hour, June-Sept., 10-4 daily and weekends, holidays and vacation time during the winter, weather permitting. Adults, $4; ages 13-17 $2.50; 5-12, $1.

Sicilian immigrant Baldasare Forestiere, a prosperous grapegrower and horticulturist, devoted his life to creating his own very individual way of life. When he decided that he couldn't bear the Fresno summer heat, he dug out a small underground room—and then kept digging until, forty years later, he had a seven-acre underground estate. Visitors wind through an amazing network of rooms, courts, patios, and passageways to view the strange and quite incredible fruit trees that Forestiere created. One tree grows seven fruits— Valencia and navel oranges, grapefruits, sweet and sour lemons, cheedro (a Sicilian rind fruit), and tangerines. Fig trees grow roots from one room to another and many more varieties—dates, pomegranates, loquats, carob trees, oriental jujubes, flowering quince, Italian pears— bend to the skylights. You'll also see Forestiere's living quarters and furnishings and the ponds in which he kept fish fresh for dinner. No one in our party finished the tour without admiration for a man who had a dream and who dedicated his life to achieving it.

BAR 20 DAIRY FARM

4260 West Madison Avenue, Fresno. (209) 264-0472. 12-5 daily. Guided tours by appointment. Free.

On your way to the Kearney mansion, stop off for a moment to see how cows are milked. The Bar 20 is a working farm, with one long gray building at the end of the driveway that is open to the public for "cow-viewing." One wall of the building is glass so you can see the cows as they line up to be washed, milked, fed, and corralled. A taped explanation tells you what's happening. In the corral outside, you can watch the calves at play.

FRESNO HISTORICAL SOCIETY MUSEUM AND M. THEO KEARNEY MANSION

7160 W. Kearney Blvd., Kearney Park, Fresno. (209) 264-8317. Wed.—Sun. 2-4:30; weekends only in Jan. and

Feb. Adults $1; 6-18 25¢.

M. Theodore Kearney, the first president of the California Raisin Growers Association, was a late nineteenth-century industrialist who lived and spent well. A guide takes you past hand-blown Tiffany lamps, photos of Mr. Kearney with his luxurious cars and his old flame, Lillie Langtry, and his office safe with a floor of concrete five feet thick. A Mother Goose book, 1908 dictionary, feather bed, and shelf of toys are in the nursery. Listen to the piano roll in the dining room and note the buzzer on the arm of Kearney's chair, which was used to page the servants. The fully furnished bedrooms, with clothes laid out, make a visitor feel that the Kearneys have just stepped out and will be back any moment. The mansion is set in a lovely park with a tea house, playgrounds and picnic areas.

ROEDING PARK ZOO AND STORYLAND

890 W. Belmont, Roeding Park, Fresno. Zoo: (209) 488-1549 and 264-5988. 10-5 daily, till 8 in summer. Over 15 years, 75¢. Storyland: 264-2235. 10-5 daily in summer; weekends in winter; closed Dec. and Jan. Over 3 years, 75¢. The park is open from 10-5 daily.

More than 550 birds, mammals and reptiles live in this neat little zoo. The aviary is green and open, with a walkway that allows you to see the birds "head-on." The door to the giraffes' shelter is marked with a scale of feet and inches so you can measure how tall the giraffes are. The seals uses a slide to swoop down into their pond. There are rare white rhinos, orangutans with babies, and a scimitar-horned oryx. You can peek into the nursery through a glass window.

In *STORYLAND*, talking storybook keys (60¢) persuade the blue caterpillar to tell eight classic fairy-tales; when the children have heard the stories, they can go on to visit the heroes of the tales. They can play in King Arthur's castle, Red Riding Hood's grandmother's cottage, Mr. Toad's cart, or they can talk to Simple Simon's pie man, the knights and knaves of Alice's court, the Three Bears, or Little Miss Muffet. They can follow the Crooked Mile, slide down Jack's beanstalk, climb Owl's tree, and have a drink at Mother Goose's fountain.

FORT MILLERTON (488-1551, 10-5 weekends, donation) is an old blockhouse that now has an exhibit of pioneer life. Visitors can see antique children's toys, the history of the lumber industry, and the complete medical kit of Fresno's first doctor.

SAN JOAQUIN FISH HATCHERY

Friant. Off Hwy. 41, seven miles northeast of Fresno. (209) 822-2374. 8-4 daily. Free.

There are more fish in this one spot than you'll ever see again: more than two million trout, in sizes that range from pinhead to fingerling to almost catchable, are raised in these trout-hatching ponds. Four times a day the fish are fed high-protein, dry pellets. When they're a year old and ten inches long, they're taken in tanks by plane and truck to the heavily fished lakes and streams of California. But while they're here, it's really fun to walk along the forty-eight ponds and watch the fish leap over and slide down the little dams between them. A photo exhibit and recorded lecture explains trout habits and the trout-seeding program.

FRIANT DAM & MILLERTON LAKE STATE RECREATIONAL AREA

Off Hwy. 41. (209) 822-2212. 9-5 daily. Tours inside by appointment.

Fed by Sierra snows, the waters of Millerton Lake are released into the Friant-Kern irrigation canals to feed the rich croplands of Fresno County. The dam is 319 feet high and 3,488 feet long with a reservoir capacity of 5,200,000 gallons. You can walk half way across the dam while guides tell you the history of the project. Millerton Lake State Recreation Area offers boating, swimming, fishing, camping, and picnic space, and the old *Millerton Courthouse*, overlooking the dam, is a pleasant little museum of Friant history (10-6 weekends, 50¢. 822-2332).

MADERA COUNTY MUSEUM

210 West Yosemite, Madera. (209) 673-0291. 1:30-4:30 weekends and by appointment. Free.

Three floors of displays emphasize the county's mining, logging and agricultural history, in the 1900 granite courthouse set in the city park. The Superior Courtroom has been restored and there's a section of the fume of the Madera Sugar Pine Lumber Company. The "downtown room" shows what the city looked like in 1900 and even has a real stagecoach.

FRESNO FLATS HISTORIC PARK

Hwy. 427, Oakhurst. (209) 683-7463.

The Sierra Historical Sites Association is restoring the 111-year-old Marge Lyman home and the original Fresno Flats Schoolhouse is being converted into the Nathan Sweet Museum to tell the story of the area and its people.

MARIPOSA COUNTY HISTORY CENTER

Library Building, Hwy. 140 at 10th Street, Mariposa. (209) 966-2924. Daily except Sun., 10-4; weekends only in winter. Free.

An Indian teepee in the front yard guides you to this gem of a museum. Inside, you'll find an 1850s street, with newspaper office, assay office, saloon, drug store, and 1850s schoolroom, each furnished as it was in Gold Rush days. A five-stamp mill that crushed gold-bearing quartz at the Golden Key mine, a hand-operated Washington Hoe printing press, and a reconstructed

Indian village will enthrall inquiring youngsters.

The nearby *Mariposa County Courthouse* (966-2005, 9-5 Mon.—Fri. and tours by appointment, free) is the oldest courthouse still in use in California. The clock in the tower has been counting time since 1866. Visitors will enjoy the "law in motion" days on the second and fourth Friday of each month and the extensive collection of Mariposa County gemstones and minerals in the halls.

YOSEMITE MOUNTAIN SUGAR PINE RAILROAD

Hwy. 41, Yosemite Mountain, Fish Camp. (209) 683-7273. 10-4 daily in summer; weekends and holidays, weather permitting in Sept. and May. Closed Nov. through April. Adults $4; ages 3-12, $2.

Just four miles from Yosemite Basin, this scenic, historic narrow-gauge steam railroad and logging train wends its way through four miles of forest, past Slab Town Loop and Honey Hill and down to the bottom of a canyon. You can stop there and have a picnic and then return on a later train.

YOSEMITE NATIONAL PARK

Enter through Fish Camp on Hwy. 41, El Portal on Hwy. 140 or Hwy. 120 (this road to Tioga Pass is closed during the winter, which may last until May). Visitor's Center: (209) 372-4461. 8-6 daily, 9-5 in spring and fall, winter, weekends, weather permitting. Museum open daily in summer only. Cars, $3 a day.

If you and your family had only one sight to see in California, your best choice would be Yosemite National Park. Yosemite is one of the world's wonders and is a world within itself for both man and nature. Elevations range from less than 2,000 to over 13,000 feet and, in these 11,000 feet, five different plant belts exist. Each sustains a part of the park's wildlife population of 220 bird and 75 mammal species. In this natural splendor you can hike, swim, camp, fish, ski, ride horseback, bicycle, or simply go sightseeing. Your first stop should be the Visitor's Center in Yosemite Valley where you can learn about the park from the center's pamphlets, exhibits, audio-visual programs, lectures, and guided walks. The *Yosemite Guide*, free, at entrance stations, gives the latest schedules. One program complete with fireside stories and toasted marshmallows was created especially for youngsters.

Where you go in Yosemite will, of course, depend on your time, interests and the time of year. You can choose from mountains, giant sequoia groves, towering waterfalls like Bridal Veil, and breathtaking vistas of Sentinel Rock and El Capitan.

There are also museums in Yosemite for rainy days or a change of pace. The *INDIAN CULTURAL CENTER* near the Visitors' Center is of interest. At the *PIONEER YOSEMITE HISTORY CENTER* at Wawona you can wander through a collection of horse-drawn vehicles, an old jail, a miner's hut, a working wagon shop, and a covered bridge. Old-time crafts demonstrations of soap-making, rail-splitting and spinning are fun, and you can talk to costumed historian-interpreters who portray the original occupants of cabins representing the different stages in the development of Yosemite National Park.

The *YOSEMITE TRAVEL MUSEUM*, in the Administration area near Arch Rock entrance, tells the story of early-day railroad and auto transportation in the Yosemite region. It has a caboose, a locomotive and a couple of cars on the grounds. The *Geology Museum* at the Visitors' Center in Yosemite Valley, shows how the mountains, waterfalls and gorges in Yosemite were formed. The natural history of Yosemite is also explored at the *Happy Isles Nature Center*.

Yosemite is always very crowded in July and August, so it is wise to plan your visit during June or September, if you can. For information about the park, write to Superintendent, Yosemite National Park, CA 95389, or telephone (209) 372-4461. Camp reservations may be made through Ticketron. Hotel reservations are a must. Call 373-4171 or contact the Yosemite Park and Curry Co., Yosemite National Park, CA 95389. For road and weather information call 372-4605.

BODIE STATE HISTORIC PARK

(13 miles east of Hwy. 395; seven miles south of Bridgeport) Bodie. Free. Accessible only in summer. Smoking is allowed in designated areas only.

Nestled high in sagebrush country, Bodie has escaped all the commercialism found in most ghost towns of the West—it doesn't even have a phone. The 170 original buildings that still stand are maintained in a state of arrested disintegration—neither restored nor allowed to decay further. You walk by the 1878 Methodist church, the windowless jail, a frame schoolhouse, a small home that belonged to President Hoover's brother, the morgue with caskets still on view, and the iron vault of the bank, which was the scene of many exciting hold-ups. Information comes from a self-guiding tour pamphlet stowed in a container on the side of a building. Just wander through this quiet, ramshackled town and imagine all the high adventures that occurred here, more than a century ago.

12

NORTH CENTRAL CALIFORNIA

The north central and northeastern area is the most rugged, remote part of Northern California, yet offers many unique and extraordinary sights. Lava Beds National Monument, Modoc National Forest and Lassen Volcanic National Park are snowed-in in winter and blazingly hot in summer. Distances between towns are long, so be sure to arrange overnight camping or lodging before you set out. Nature lovers will enjoy the Whiskeytown-Lake Shasta-Trinity area and McArthur Burney Falls Memorial State Park—and all the wonderful open spaces whose very inaccessibility make them places to aim for.

COMMUNITY MEMORIAL MUSEUM

1333 Butte House Road, Yuba City. (916) 674-0461. Mon.–Fri. 9-5; Sat. 1-4. Free.

This small community museum houses artifacts of the Indians and early pioneers of Sutter County, as well as exhibits on the natural history of the area. Baskets and beads, grinding pots, and a skeleton represent the local Indians, while antique pianos lugged around Cape Horn, family books and Bibles and everyday clothing and dishes depict pioneer life. Mementos from the Chinese settlers are also included. But the starring item in the collection is Lola Montez' dressing table, surely one of the "tools" of this dazzling actress and seductress.

In Marysville, Yuba's Sister City, an 1857 family residence has become a museum, the *Mary Aaron Memorial Museum* at 704 D Street (Tues.–Sat.,

1:30-4:30 p.m. Tours by appointment for fourth graders and older. Free. (916) 743-1004) with the original furniture and clothing and an interesting display of dolls, documents and photographs. Our favorite artifact is an 1860s wedding cake that was discovered perfectly intact and petrified in a wooden Wells Fargo storage box.

SACRAMENTO VALLEY MUSEUM

1495 E Street, Hwy. 20, at Inter. 5, Williams. (916) 473-5423. Fri.–Wed. 10-5. Adults, 50¢; children 25¢.

A general store, a blacksmith shop and saddlery, an apothecary shop, a barber shop, and restored early California rooms are included in this twenty-one-room museum that is filled with memories. The doll collection dates from Mycenaean times and there's even an 1800 newspaper reporting President George Washington's death. The double cradle from the 1700s is also special.

OROVILLE CHINESE TEMPLE

1500 Broderick, Oroville. (916) 533-1496. Fri.–Tues. 10-12 and 1-4:30 in winter, 1-4:30 Wed. and Thurs. as well in summer. Ages 12 and older, $1; tours of 15 or more 75¢ each.

This complex of Buddhist, Taoist and Confucian temples houses one of the finest collections of Chinese artifacts in the U.S. At the door of one building stands a two-ton, cast-iron urn, given to the temple by Emperor Quong She. Carved teakwood altars, old tapestries, gods and goddesses, dragons, rare lanterns and shrines are found throughout the buildings. The Moon Temple,

used for Buddhist worship is entered through a circular doorway, which symbolizes the circle of life. The arts and lives of the thousands of Chinese who migrated to the gold fields are wonderfully reflected in this peaceful spot.

Nearby is the *Lott House Museum* at 1607 Montgomery St. (916/533-7699, Fri.–Tues. 10:30-12 and 1-4:30, $1). Once the home of Judge C. F. Lott, this nineteenth-century house is furnished with period pieces and early American art.

The *Oroville Pioneer Museum*, further up Montgomery St. (916/534-0198, 1-4 Sun. and by appointment, donation) is a grand collection of pioneer memorabilia including early typewriters, an old fire engine, pictures of the Oroville floods, and a facsimile miner's cabin.

FEATHER RIVER FISH HATCHERY AND OROVILLE DAM

5 Table Mountain Blvd., Oroville. (916) 534-2465. Hatchery: 8-6 daily. Dam overlook (534-2324) 8 a.m.-9 p.m. May-Sept.; 8-8 Oct. and Nov.; 8-5 Dec.-April. Free.

A large window in the hatchery enables visitors to see the salmon climb the fish ladder to spawn (usually in September). Over 10,000 salmon and steelhead make their homes here now. Ten miles down the road, you can get a good view of the 770-foot dam across the Feather River.

BIDWELL MANSION

Chico State College, 525 Esplanade, Chico. (916)

895-6144. 10-4 daily, except holidays. Adults, 50¢. 45 min. guided tours every hour on the hour.

Rancho Chico, covering 26,000 acres, was purchased in 1849 by agriculturist and politician John Bidwell. His large Victorian home soon became the social and cultural center of the upper Sacramento Valley. Bidwell's is a California success story. His first job was as a clerk for John Sutter, then majordomo, and soon an officer in the Mexican War. After that, he set himself up at Chico and built a model farm. He raised corn, oats, barley, peaches, pears, apples, figs, quince, almonds, walnuts, sugar cane, olives, and casaba melons. He was elected state senator and congressman, and even ran for President. Visitors may walk through the graciously furnished rooms, among which the library with its wicker sidechairs, tea cart, unique fireplace screen and weaving table, is special. Children will like the cabinet of stuffed birds in the General's office and the intricate Victorian hair wreaths in the parlor. Bidwell Park, third largest municipal park in the nation, was also part of the Bidwell estate.

The nearby *Stansbury Home* (5th and Salem, 343-4401 x236, 1-4, Sat. and Sun., Adults 75¢, children 50¢), an 1883 Italianate Victorian filled with period furnishings, is remarkable because only Stansburys have lived in it and it has never been remodeled or modernized.

SOUTH SHASTA LINES

G.A. Humann Ranch. Tehama Road, Gerber. (916) 385-1389. Open even-numbered years in April and May on Sunday from 1-4, by appointment. Adults $2; under 12 $1.

Fire boxes glow in the locomotives and the mailman catches mailbags tossed from a speeding train. Signs blink, bells ring and railroad fans sigh nostalgically as the miniature wood-burning engine toots along. Twelve steam locomotives and ninety cars, all built to scale, operate along 840 feet of track. A railroad museum and old-time farm machinery display is on the ranch. In odd-numbered years, there's a Steam Threshing Bee with parade and demonstrations, on Labor Day weekends.

WILLIAM B. IDE ADOBE SHP

1 mile north of Red Bluff on Adobe Road. (916) 527-5927. 8-5 daily. Free.

"He hereby invites all good and patriotic citizens in California to assist him—to establish and perpetuate a liberal, a just and honorable government, which shall secure to all civil, religous and personal liberty." So wrote William B. Ide to introduce the Bear Flag Republic to California. As first President of the Bear Flag Republic, he helped bring California into the Union. But when the Republic failed, Ide went to the gold fields and then returned home to his adobe, which also served as a ferry station between Sacramento and Shasta's Northern Gold Mines. The house is small and unassuming, with family photos, cradle and high chair, a furnished kitchen and an unusual sleeping platform under the eaves. A smokehouse and a carriage house, with covered wagons, buggies and Ide's branding equipment, are also open to the public. Two three-hundred-year-old oaks lead the way to another small museum that includes gold-mining tools, an old button collection and a well-used cribbage board.

In Red Bluff, the *Kelly-Griggs House Museum* (311

Washington St., 527-1129) is open for old house buffs, Thurs.–Sun., 2-5. Donation.

RED BLUFF DIVERSION DAM AND SPAWNING FACILITY

Williams Ave. & Sale Lane, Red Bluff. (916) 527-7440. 8-4 daily. Free.

The world's largest artificial salmon-spawning channel includes closed-circuit cameras for watching the fish moving through the channels. An interpretive center explains what you're seeing. Movies on the migrating Chinooks and a glass viewing wall for watching the salmon helps, too. Salmon runs are heaviest from October to mid-December, when you can see the fish traversing the fish ladder.

Fish hatchery buffs might like to ride to Anderson, six miles off Highway 5, above Red Bluff, to see the *COLEMAN NATIONAL FISH HATCHERY* (365-8622, 8-4:30 daily, free), the world's largest chinook salmon plant. Every year, thirty to forty million salmon and steelhead eggs are hatched, then raised to catchable size in this hatchery. Spawning takes place in the fall, but there's always something to see here. For information on other hatcheries in California, call (916) 275-1589.

CARTER HOUSE SCIENCE MUSEUM

1701 Rio Drive, Redding. (916) 244-0622. Wed.–Fri. 12-4:30, Sat. and Sun. 10-4. Free.

Did you know that tarantulas enjoy walking along your arm? In the petting section of this lively junior science museum, you can pet a tarantula—or a possum or ground squirrel. Native animals that are injured—sparrow hawks, screech owls, California boa constrictors—and domestic animals are cared for here. Free nature and science films on weekends and special programs such as moon rock displays keep the place jumping.

REDDING MUSEUM AND ART CENTER

1911 Rio Drive, Caldwell Park, Redding. (916) 243-4994. 10-5 daily except Mon. in summer, Tues.–Fri. and Sun. 12-5 and Sat. 10-5 in winter. Free. Closed holidays.

A fantastic doll collection—featuring a Shirley Temple doll, an 1850 papier-mâché doll, a 1904 tin doll and 1908 *Ladies' Home Journal* paper dolls—is just one of the revolving exhibits in this excellent museum. Carousel animals is another, as are changing art shows and historical exhibits. The story of Pomo Indian basketry—from cradle, to pots, dresses, luggage and houses, to gifts for the funeral pyre—is remarkable. The permanent Indian and primitive collections include pre-Columbian pottery, canoe prows from the Trobriand Islands and "wife beaters" from the Australian aborigines. Crafts and baskets from the Hoopa, Karok, Yurok, Wintu, Zuni, Yaqui, and Hopi Indians are nicely presented.

SHASTA

Hwy. 299 west of Redding. Old Shasta (916) 243-8194. 10-5 daily. Adults, 50¢.

Once the center of the rich northern gold mines, Shasta is now a quiet ghost town in the process of being restored. The old county courthouse contains a remarkable collection of California art along with displays of photographs and relics of the Indians, Chinese, gold miners, and pioneers who once lived here. Modoc handicrafts, Chinese wooden pillows and money, an 1879 *Godey's Ladies Book* and the pistol John Brown used in his raid at Harper's Ferry are a few of the highlights. The courtroom is furnished as it was when in use and the jail is still equipped with chains, leg irons and a gallows. The Litsch Miners' Supply Store, open in summer, looks just as it did in the 1860s, with barrels of meat and wine, old hats, and picks and shovels for sale. Picnic areas are available near the barn and stagecoach.

J. J. (JAKE) JACKSON MEMORIAL MUSEUM AND TRINITY COUNTY HISTORICAL PARK

Main Street, Hwy. 299W, Weaverville. (916) 623-5211. 10-5 daily, May-Nov. Free.

Museum displays trace Trinity County's history from the days of the Indian through the gold-mining years. Ray Jackson's collection of antique firearms, an 1849 fire wagon, Chinese tong war weapons, and reconstructed miner's cabin and blacksmith shop help to recall this bygone era.

WEAVERVILLE CHINESE JOSS HOUSE

Hwy. 299W, Weaverville. (916) 623-5284. 10-5 daily, except holidays; Adults, 50¢.

Tours every hour on the hour in winter, on the half hour in summer. The Temple of the Forest and the Clouds is open for worship now, as it has been since 1853. A small museum displays Chinese art, mining tools, weapons used in the tong wars and photos of Chinese Laborers building the railroads. A Lion Dance headdress, an abacus, opium pipes, and a huge gong are also shown. Inside the temple, you see the paper money that is burned for the gods and the drum and bell that wake the gods so they'll hear your prayers. In the rear of the temple, the attendants' quarters are furnished as they were one hundred years ago, with bunk beds and wooden pillows. Colorful altars, temple saints, celebration drums and flags and the mirror-covered king's umbrella that guarded him against evil spirits create a vivid picture of the religion and its people.

IRONSIDE MUSEUM

Hawkins Bar, on Hwy. 299W near Burnt Ranch. (916) 629-2396. By chance or by appt. Donation.

Ray Nachand shares his personal collection daily in summer and irregularly in winter. Pioneer artifacts include butter churns, doctor's instruments, guns, a

Weaverville Joss House.

collection of two hundred padlocks, a glass insulator collection, Mrs. Nachand's carnival glass collection, and high-button shoes. Assaying equipment, mining equipment, machinery, and a blacksmith shop share the bill with gold that Mr. Nachand has mined.

HOOPA TRIBAL MUSEUM

Hoopa Shopping Center, Hwy 96 (off 299W), Hoopa. (916) 625-4110. 10-5, Mon.–Fri. in winter, 10-6 daily in summer. Free.

Stone implements, dishes, tools, baskets, and dance regalia of the Hoopa Indians—named by Jedediah Smith's Yurok guide as "the people who live up the river"—are shown here, along with items from other tribes such as Kachina dolls from the Southwest and Alaskan, and Canadian baskets. Many of the Hoopa items are on loan from local residents and from the

Smithsonian Institution and the Lowie Museum of Anthropology in Berkeley. There's also a showcase of mementos from the gold mining era and the artifacts discovered by crews working in the Six Rivers National Forest.

SHASTA DAM

Hwy. 15 off Interstate 5. (916) 275-2420/241-6584. 9-5 daily in summer; films at 10, 12 and 2 daily in winter. Free.

Deer come to be fed by children when the lights shine on Shasta Dam at night. During the day, the 602-foot dam, second highest in the world, is an even more spectacular sight. Snow-capped Mount Shasta (which is climbable) looms in the distance accentuating the differences between natural and man-made wonders. A self-guided tour and a model and film explain how the dam works. Jet-boat tours, houseboating, and every kind of water sport are popular in this Whiskeytown-Shasta-Trinity National Recreation Area. *SCOTT'S MUSEUM*, in Trinity Center is open daily, 10-5, in summer and features items of local history.

LAKE SHASTA CAVERNS

Off Lake Shasta in O'Brien. (916) 238-2341. Two-hour tours throughout the day, including a 15-minute catamaran ride across the lake, from 8 a.m. in summer, at 10, 12 and 2 in winter. Adults, $5, children 5-15, $3.

Discovered in 1878 by J. A. Richardson (you can still see his inscription), the Lake Shasta Caverns are a natural wonder. Stalactite and stalagmite formations range from the eight-inch high "Ballerina" to the sixty-foot "Cathedral Room" of stalactite draperies that are studded with crystals. Multicolored formations unfold before you during your tour, as you hear fact and Wintu Indian legend from a knowledgeable guide.

SISKIYOU COUNTY MUSEUM

910 South Main St., Yreka. (916) 842-3836. 9-5 daily in summer, closed Mondays, holidays and Sundays, 1-5 in winter. Free.

The story of the Siskiyou County is told in seven periods—Prehistoric, Indian, Trapper, Gold Rush, Transportation, Industry, and Progress. The museum is a reproduction of the old Callahan Ranch Hotel (1854), the first stage stop in the county. Dishes, silver, dolls, photographs, diaries, and clothing of the pioneers are on the mezzanine. The basement displays a completely furnished country store, a miner's cabin, a milliner's shop and gun, mineral and Indian exhibits. Tree fossils, relics from the Hudson's Bay trappers and the huge shell of the eupachydiscus shellfish, sixty million years old, are of special interest.

Nearby, *THE COUNTY COURT HOUSE* at Fouth and Lane Streets (916/842-3531, Mon.–Fri. 8-5) displays gold nuggets, panned gold, placer gold, and local gemstones.

LAVA BEDS NATIONAL MONUMENT

Off Hwy. 139, near Tulelake. (916) 667-2601. Camping, $3, in summer only.

Natural and Indian history vie for the visitor's

Old Shasta lives again!

attention in this monumental landscape created by black lava from the earth's crust. The area abounds with natural wonders, including cinder cones that reach up as high as five hundred feet. Lava running underground has shaped hundreds of caves which can be explored with care. The Merrill Ice Caves contain a still river and a waterfall formed of ice. Another is decorated with drawings by the Indians who once lived here. Captain Jack's Stronghold, a fort fashioned of lava, is a grim reminder of later history: in 1872, Captain Jack led a band of Modoc Indians in a bloody but unsuccessful uprising against the U.S. Cavalry. This was the only Indian war in California. A short visit to monument headquarters (open 8-5 in summer, 8-4:30 when weather permits in winter) will help you understand the geology, natural history and past events of the area.

ALTURAS MODOC CO. HISTORICAL MUSEUM

600 S. Main, Alturas. (916) 233-2944. May 1-Nov. 1, 9-4 weekdays, 10-4:30 weekends. Free.

To learn more about Captain Jack, and see pictures of him, go to this pleasant museum in the far corner of the state. There are beads, baskets, arrowheads and other Indian artifacts along with pioneer memorabilia. The collections of stuffed birds and antique guns are visitors' favorites.

WILLIAM H. PRATT MEMORIAL MUSEUM AND ROOPS' FORT

75 N. Weatherlow Street, Susanville. (916) 257-5721. 10-4 daily, May 15-Nov. 15. Free.

Lassen County memorabilia, farming and lumbering machinery, artifacts of the native Americans and remembrances of the first settlers, Isaac Roops and Peter Lassen, fill this interesting museum. You can peek through the fence of next-door Roops' Fort, built in 1854 as the first building in Lassen County, to see wagon wheels from the Donner Party. Susanville is named after the daughter of Isaac Roops, Governor of the Provisional Territory of Nevada and Nataqua.

LASSEN VOLCANIC NATIONAL PARK

Hwy. 36, Mineral. Info. centers at Manzanita Lake and Sulphur Works open from early June to late Sept. (916) 595-4444. Road closed in winter.

Caves, hot springs, boiling pools, mud pots, sparkling lakes, and the cinder cone which erupted in 1851 are visitor attractions in this rugged area. An Indian lore program at park headquarters tells the story and customs of the Yana, Yahi, Mountain Maidu and Atsugewi Indians who once lived here. Ishi, story-book hero and last man of the Yahi tribe, was found near here and the photos of him living with his customs in a modern world are interesting. Indians of other tribes still sell baskets and tell stories on the campgrounds. One note of warning: the grounds and thermal areas are treacherous, so keep hold of your children at all times. Lassen Peak erupted for seven years beginning in May, 1914, and it's due for another blow soon.

PUBLIC RELATIONS TOURS

PACIFIC COAST PRODUCERS. Oroville. (916) 533-4311. Free tours by appointment in Aug. and Sept. to see fruit cocktail, peaches, and tomatoes canned.

LIBBY CANNERY. 100 Virginia St., Gridley. (916) 846-5621. Free. By appointment. Libby cans peaches in July and August.

DEL MONTE. B and Plumas Streets, Yuba City. (916) 673-4179. Make an appointment to see the canning process from fruit to case for cling peaches.

RUMIANO CHEESE CO. Country Road F, Willows. (916) 934-5438. Tours, arranged by appointment, will see the packaging and cutting of huge dry jack wheels, Monterey Jack, pepper jack, and seven other cheeses.

13

SPECIAL ANNUAL EVENTS

JANUARY

San Francisco Sports & Boat Show, Cow Palace.
San Mateo Auto Show, Fairgrounds.
Harlem Globe Trotters, Oakland Coliseum.
Golden Gate Kennel Club All-Breed Dog Show, San Francisco.
Four-Dog Sled Races, Prosser Lake and Donner Lake.
Whale watching begins, Pt. Reyes National Seashore.
Fiddler's Contest & Crab Cioppino Feed, Cloverdale.

FEBRUARY

Chinese New Years Celebration, San Francisco.
Athens Track Meet.
National Road Show, Oakland Coliseum.
Crab Festival, Crescent City.
Crab Cioppino Feast, Bodega Bay.
Redwood Region Logging Conference, Eureka.
Chinese Bomb Day, Bok Kai Festival, Marysville.
Cloverdale Citrus Fair (third weekend).
Clam Beach Run, Trinidad.
Carnival & Spring Fair, Lakeport.
California Special Olympics Winter Games, Sonora.

MARCH

Camellia Show, Santa Rosa.
Crab Feed, Ukiah.
Pixie Parents Easter Fair, Ross.
Draggin' Wagins Dance Festival, Sonora.
Sierra Dog Sled Races, Sierra City, Truckee and Ebbets Pass.
Candlefishing at Night, Klamath River.
Fresno Camellia Show.
Junior Grand National Livestock Expo, Cow Palace, San Francisco.
Jackass Mail Run, Porterville (or first weekend in April).
Cherry Blossom Festival, Japantown, San Francisco (or early April).

APRIL

Log Race, Petaluma River.
Fisherman's Festival, Bodega Bay.
Baseball season opens.
Annual Trinidad Crab Feed.
Gem & Mineral Show, Cow Palace, San Francisco.
Yacht Parade, Redwood City.

Clovis Rodeo.
Carmel Kite Festival.
Gold Nugget Days, Paradise.
Children's Lawn Festival, Redding.
Red Bluff Romp & Rodeo.
Coalinga Water Festival.
Nikkei Matsuri Festival, San Jose.
Apple Blossom Festival, Sebastopol.
Fresno Folk Festival.
Rhododendron Festival, Eureka.
Boonville Buck-A-Roo Days.
Calaveras County Jumping Frog Jubilee, Angels Camp.

MAY

Laguna Seca Races, Scramp, Monterey.
Cinco de Mayo Festivals in San Francisco and San Jose.
Opening Day Yacht Parade, San Francisco.
Ferndale Arts Festival.
Avenue of the Giants Marathon, Garberville.
Bay to Breakers Race, San Francisco.
Luther Burbank Rose Festival, Santa Rosa.
Mendocino Art Fair.
Mt. Folk Festival, Potter Valley.
West Coast National Antique Fly-in, Watsonville Airport.
Salinas Valley Fair, King City.
West Coast Relays, Fresno.
Chamarita Festival and Parade, Half Moon Bay (Pentecost Sunday).
Chamarita Festival and Parade, Sausalito (Pentecost Sunday).
Old Settlers Day, Campbell.

Fireman's Muster, Columbia.
Lamb Derby Days, Willow.
Russian River Wine Festival, Healdsburg.
Stump Town Days and Rodeo, Guerneville (or early June).
Coarsegold Rodeo, Madera County.
Fiddletown Gold Country Hoedown.
Prospector's Daze, Willow Creek.

JUNE

Black Bart Celebration, Redwood Valley.
Sonoma/Marin Fair, Petaluma Fairgrounds.
Upper Grant Avenue Street Fair, San Francisco.
Fly-In & Moonlight Flight, Porterville.
Alameda County Fair, Pleasanton.
Merienda, Monterey's birthday party.
San Antonio Mission Fiesta, Jolon.
Springfest, San Mateo Fairgrounds.
Old Auburn Flea Market.
Italian Picnic and Parade, Sutter Creek.
Klamath Salmon barbecue.
Shasta Brigade Jamboree, Redding.
Malakoff Home-Coming, Nevada City.
Solano County Fair, Vallejo.
Novato County Fair.
Pony Express Days, McKinleyville.
Garberville Rodeo and Western Celebration.
San Francisco Kite Festival.
Bear Flag Day, Sonoma.
Tuolumne Jubilee, Tuolumne City.
Days of Kit Carson, Jackson.
Middletown Days.

Bonanza Days, Gilroy.
Redwood Acres Fair, Eureka.
Western Daze, Fairfield.
Western Weekend, Novato.
Swedish Festival, Kingsburg (second Sat.).
Vaquero Days, Hollister.
Horse Show & Rodeo, San Benito.
Midsummer Music Festival, Sigmund Stern Grove, San
    Francisco (through August).
Highway 50 Wagon Train, Placerville.
Secession Day, Rough & Ready (June 27).
San Francisco's Birthday Celebration.

JULY

Old Time 4th of July Celebration, Columbia.
Salmon B-B-Q, Noyo.
Sonoma County Fair, Santa Rosa.
C.B. Radio Convention, Eureka.
Bach Festival, Carmel.
California Rodeo, Salinas.
Nihon Machi Street Fair, San Francisco.
Asian Festival, Oakland Museum.
Hoopa Fourth of July Celebration.
Pony Express Celebration, Pollack Pines.
Napa County Fair, Calistoga (July 4th).
Willits Frontier Days (4th of July).
Arcata Salmon Festival.
Mendota Sugar Jamboree.
Garberville Rodeo.
San Mateo County Fair.
Woodminster Music Series, Oakland (through
    September).

Old-Fashioned Fourth, Mt. Shasta.
Old-Fashioned Fourth, Crescent City.
Dune Daze, Samoa.
Grand Comedy Festival, Eureka.
Fortuna Rodeo.
Water Carnival, Monte Rio.
Jeepers Jamboree, Georgetown to Lake Tahoe.
Fiesta Rodeo de San Juan Bautista.
Captain Weber Days, Stockton.
OBON Festival, Monterey.
OBON Festival, Fresno.
Scotts Valley Days.
Gold Rush Jubilee, Callahan, Siskiyou County.
Feast of Lanterns, Pacific Grove.
Orick Rodeo.
Easter Lily Festival, Smith River.
Gasket Raft Races.
Turtle Races, Cloverdale.
Nightboat Parade, Lakeport and Clearlake Highlands.

AUGUST

Old Adobe Days, Petaluma.
Monterey County Fair.
Humboldt County Fair, Ferndale.
Dipsea Foot Race, Mill Valley.
Calif. State Horseman's American Horse Show, Sonoma.
"Annie & Mary Day," Blue Lake.
Santa Clara County Fair, San Jose.
Gilroy Garlic Festival.
Wildwood Days & Peddlers' Faire, Rio Dell.
Siskiyou County Fair and Paul Bunyan Jubilee.
Ringling Brothers Circus, Oakland.

El Dorado Days at Mt. Ranch, San Andreas.
Mother Lode Fair and Loggers' Contest, Sonora.
Plumas County Fair, Quincy.
Pony Express Day, McKinleyville (Aug. 22).
Children's Fairyland Birthday Week, Oakland.
Air Round-Up, Red Bluff.
Willow Creek Bigfoot Days.
Del Norte County Fair, Crescent City.
Gravenstein Apple Fair, Sebastopol.
Lake County Fair, Lakeport.
Marin County Fair, San Rafael.

SEPTEMBER

Sausalito Art Festival.
Begonia Festival, Capitola.
Monterey Jazz Festival.
Renaissance Faire, Novato.
Mendocino County Fair & Apple Show, Boonville.
Ringling Brothers Circus, San Francisco.
San Francisco Art Festival.
Fall Festival, Japantown, San Francisco.
Redwood Empire Logging Festival, McKinleyville.
Constitution Days, Nevada City.
Vintage Festival, Hall of Flowers, Golden Gate Park, San Francisco.
California State Fair, Sacramento.
Scottish Games, Santa Rosa Fairgrounds.
Pageant of Fire Mountain, Guerneville.
Vintage Car Fair, Fremont.
National Indian Observance Day, Crescent City.
American Indian Day, Volcano.
Paul Bunyan Days, Fort Bragg.

Santa Cruz County Fair, Watsonville.
Salinas Rodeo.
Vintage Festival, Sonoma.
Northcountry Fair, Arcata.
Carmel Mission Fiesta.
Fiesta del Pueblo, San Jose.
Redwood Invitational Regatta, Big Lagoon, Humboldt County.
Oktoberfest, San Mateo Fairgrounds.
Oktoberfest, San Jose.
Lodi Grape Festival.
Fiesta Patrias, Woodland.
Castroville Artichoke Festival.
Walnut Festival, Walnut Creek.
Sonoma Valley of the Moon Festival.

OCTOBER

Laguna Seca Grand Prix, Monterey.
Fortuna Arts Festival.
Sonoma County Harvest Festival, Santa Rosa.
Fresno Fair.
National Livestock Expo, San Francisco.
Marin Grape Festival, San Rafael.
Pumpkin Festival, Half Moon Bay.
Football season starts.
Spanishtown Art & Pumpkin Festival.
Candle Lighter Ghost House, Fremont.
Pro-Am Surfing International Santa Cruz.
Redding Children's Art Festival.
Fall Festival, Clearlake Oaks.
Selma Parade and Band Festival.
Blessing of the Fleet, San Francisco.

Old Timers' Day, King City.
Columbus Day Festival, San Carlos.
Columbus Day Festival, San Francisco.
Reedley Festival.
Chinese Double Ten Celebration, San Francisco.
San Francisco International Film Festival.
Discovery Day, Bodega Bay.
Harvest Hoedown, Healdsburg.

NOVEMBER

North California Boat and Sports Show, Oakland.
Christmas Balloon Parade, San Jose (day after
  Thanksgiving).
Thanksgiving Art Fair, Mendocino.

DECEMBER

Christmas Art and Music Festival, Eureka.
Great Dickens Faire, San Francisco.
Nutcracker Suite, San Francisco Ballet.
Nutcracker Suite, Oakland Ballet.
Festival of the Trees, Monterey.
Festival of the Trees, San Rafael.
Shriners East-West Football Game, Candlestick Park,
  San Francisco (Dec. 31).
Lighting of the Tree of Lebanon, Santa Rosa.
New Year's Eve Fireman's Ball, Cloverdale.
Natives Christmas Tree Ceremony, Sequoia National
  Forest.
Christmas Tree Lane, Fresno.

INDEX

Photo Credits